The communicator's craft

THE COMMUNICATOR'S CRAFT

Getting your message across

James Rye

Inter-Varsity Press

INTER-VARSITY PRESS
38 De Montfort Street, Leicester LE1 7GP, England

Unless otherwise stated, Scripture quotations in this publication are from
the Holy Bible, New International Version. Copyright © 1973, 1978, 1984
International Bible Society. Published in Great Britain by Hodder and
Stoughton Ltd.

First published 1990

British Library Cataloguing in Publication Data
Rye, James
   The communicator's craft.
   1. Christianity. Communication
   I. Title
   261

ISBN 0–85110–689–7

Set in Linotron Ehrhardt

Typeset in Great Britain by Parker Typesetting Service, Leicester

Printed and bound in Great Britain by
Cox & Wyman Ltd, Reading

*Inter-Varsity Press is the book-publishing division of the Universities and Colleges
Christian Fellowship (formerly the Inter-Varsity Fellowship), a student movement
linking Christian Unions in universities and colleges throughout the United
Kingdom and the Republic of Ireland, and a member movement of the
International Fellowship of Evangelical Students. For information about local and
national activities write to UCCF, 38 De Montfort Street, Leicester LE1 7GP.*

Contents

Preface

This book arose for two reasons. First, I became increasingly suspicious of two 'doctrines' that I was being encouraged to believe by sincere teachers of the Word of God. As a young Christian I had been given the distinct impression that preaching was an extremely mysterious and even mystical activity which was virtually out of the preacher's control. As you went into the pulpit, all you could do was pray that the fire would fall. If it did (and you weren't consumed) it was good, and if it didn't, it was bad. I was also left in no doubt that you were either 'gifted' or you weren't. There seemed to be little room for developing any gifts from seeds that God may have planted. However, as I grew in my understanding and appreciation of God as a communicator, as I studied both education and communication theory, and as I practised professionally as teacher and lecturer, I began to see some principles of effective communication that removed some of the mystique of preaching. I still long for the fire to fall, but I now have a clearer understanding of my own responsibility to be a skilled craftsman.

Secondly, as someone with a professional interest in training communicators, I became appalled at the way in which many churches fail to train their speakers. Some of the large denominations obviously have very good support and training systems, but there are also large numbers of churches that provide little, if any, training. Many people are thrown in at the deep end, praised if they are natural swimmers, and criticized if they sink. And even where training is given, emphasis is often placed on content of talks, and little on communication of messages. My experience of helping some speakers and of supervising probationary teachers has convinced me that some communication skills can be developed, provided that an honest and supportive framework is given.

Although I have referred to 'preachers', I have deliberately tried to look at different types of communication in churches. There are already many good books on sermon construction, and although there will obviously be some overlap with material in such books, I hope that this book will provide fresh insights that will be applicable to a wider variety of communication situations.

In addition to learning from experience and from books, my own understanding of the communicator's craft has been influenced by two other sources. Many church communicators have stimulated my thinking and made me want to 'stir up' my own gift. I have learned a lot from listening to the effective communication of David Middleton (Norwich), Roger Carswell (itinerant evangelist), and David Oxley (formerly of King's Lynn). Although they cannot be held responsible for the ideas in this book, they have taught me much by their example. I am also grateful to friends who have encouraged me with this book and provided feedback about my own communication 'successes' and 'failures'. I am genuinely indebted to my wife, Nina, who has helped create space for teaching and writing and who has provided honest evaluation over a number of years. Her skilful and creative eye has also lovingly examined each one of my many words.

I write as one who is still travelling and *not* as one who has arrived. I am praying that this book will help you on your journey.

King's Lynn, Norfolk   *James Rye*
November 1989

CHAPTER *1*

WHY WORRY ABOUT COMMUNICATION?

Overview

Some Christians shy away from slick, salesman-like preachers. Because of bad experiences we may well think: 'I don't want to be like that. And anyway, does technique really make a difference? Isn't God in complete control? Why not just leave it to him?' The first two chapters do not advocate slickness, but they do argue that we should be concerned to communicate well.

- Chapter 1 begins by looking at our experience as listeners.
- It considers the limitations of technique.
- Chapter 2 shows that to be concerned with communication is thoroughly biblical.

Our experience of good and bad communication

If you doubt the importance of communication technique, just think about what hours of going to church may have taught you.

- How often have you allowed your mind to wander because you became tired of trying to follow the ramblings of a speaker?
- How often have you been hurt, not so much by what someone said, but by the way she or he said it?
- How often has your heart sunk after the first few sentences of a sermon, never to rise again for another half-hour at least?
- How often have you picked up some church literature and thought: 'I would be embarrassed to give this to my friends'?

Regardless of content we instinctively know when we're facing communication that makes us want to listen further or read on. There *is* a difference between good and bad. That difference can be crucial in determining how much attention we pay to a message. Unless we receive the message with care we won't understand: if we don't understand we certainly won't remember or obey. The communicator has a vital role to play in helping us want to take his or her message.

Of course, on some occasions you knew you were to blame for the communication failure. You had been up late the night before, had argued with the family on the way to church, and were in no state physically, mentally, or spiritually to receive any teaching. And then, on that particular day, the speaker *would* choose some such theme as sacrifice, which probably meant that you would be looking for an excuse to reject the message. That slight note of brutal sarcasm in the speaker's tone was all that you needed to ignite the irate flames that reduced the message to ashes.

But, on the other hand, on some occasions at least, you had been one of the committed ones. You had really wanted to understand, to listen, to learn, to receive, to participate. You had been hungry and wanted feeding. It had cost you to be there. The attraction of the beach had been real.

In your better moments you had felt sorry. At least the speaker had meant well. Perhaps the sorrow began to turn inwards and grow into frustration. It was like one of those nightmares where you find yourself running but unable to move forward – all the effort but no progress. Occasionally that frustration blossomed into anger and resentment (kept carefully hidden beneath a socially conditioned smile). How dare he waste your time? Why does nobody tell her that she's jumping around with her points? He's incoherent! Doesn't she know that she's being superficial and irrelevant? Why is he so boring?

When you calmed down there was usually the guilt to face – guilt at your own feelings, and because of your over-developed sensitivity and willingness to blame yourself. If only you had been more holy, more prayerful, more attentive, more . . ., the message would have got through.

How often have you been through all that? At least once you've been to a Christian meeting and come back numbed or empty; and at least once you've come home angry and frustrated.

Fortunately not all Christian communication is bleak. If it were our churches would be even emptier and our evangelism even less effective.

We know from our experience as either listeners or speakers that communication is never totally effective. As listeners we know that there are parts of the message that interest, inform, and even move us; there are also parts that we struggle to register. As speakers we can sense from the glazed eyes, fixed smiles, or snores that we lost them at the fourth, fourteenth or fortieth point.

Of course, there are also occasions when the communication is very effective. The majesty of God somehow seems to make the words glow as they burn into us. We don't need encouragement to listen; it's almost as if we can't stop listening. We hear a forty-five-minute sermon and feel that we've been listening for ten minutes. The message is so clear that we not only grasp the points immediately, but we can also see their relevance to our lives. For days, weeks, months, even years we can remember much of what was said on that occasion.

Then there are the less dramatic times. The communication is less traumatic for us personally, but it is still very

11

effective. It may not move us *every* week, but it doesn't bore or frustrate us. We enjoy listening to the speaker regardless of difficult content. Over the months our minds are renewed. Old concepts are regularly and graciously challenged; some good ones are given a firmer base; some bad ones are slowly but systematically destroyed while new ones are carefully erected to replace them.

> *There is a difference between the bad and the good,*
> *and we instinctively know that it is worth aiming*
> *for the best.*

Enter God (a necessary perspective)

Couldn't we just list some do's and dont's that would guide us in our communicating? Just as there's more to getting married than mere ritual and technique, there's a lot more to Christian communication than a set of rules derived from educational and social psychology.

Theology is bigger than psychology and we can't continue without bringing God into the discussion. I'm writing about Christian communication and not just about the communication of ordinary human messages. I'm concerned with helping win people for Christ and with building his church. In this book, I'm not too interested with rallying troops or selling double-glazing (although there will inevitably be some common ground). When everything that can be said about communication from a psychological perspective has been said, there is still much more that a Christian would need to say.

God created people and thus their psychological processes. He knows everything there is to know about how individuals respond to human messages. Because he made us he knows that we naturally respond to smiles, and that we can gain most from clearly structured messages in familiar language patterns. On many occasions God will choose to use natural bridges into people's understanding that good communicators can employ. But we can't say that God will always use those bridges. Sometimes he will choose to reach people in ways that bypass normal routes. He is God and he can do that. However frustrating it may seem for the aspiring communicator, God is not limited to using the norms of human behaviour and there is no automatic correlation between technique and effectiveness.

The art of persuading people to forsake one set of beliefs and one way of life, and to take up an alien set of values and a new lifestyle, cannot be reduced to a set of written rules like those offered in introductory books on car maintenance, gardening, and cooking. There are two reasons for this. First, people are more complex than machines (even your car), more mysterious than gardens (even your hedge), and more unpredictable than cooking (even your soufflé). Secondly, apart from the human element, all Christian communication has to involve the supernatural. In seeking to gain a hearing we are not facing a battle on the same level as that faced by the ordinary communicator.

We have a life-changing, eternity-fixing content; we will be engaged in a battle in which God himself will be fighting, resisting, challenging, and ultimately defeating satanic opposition. Sometimes God will work through us, and on other occasions he will speak in spite of us. No book could ever equate human technique with spiritual effectiveness. I am not trying to do that, although I sadly suspect that some superficial readers may accuse me of attempting such a doomed task.

During the second half of the last century, C. H. Spurgeon was one of the most prolific, skilful, and effective Christian communicators in the church. Ironically Spurgeon was brought to faith in Christ under the ministry of a man who, by normal standards, would be considered a very poor speaker. Look at Spurgeon's own account.

One Sunday morning Spurgeon was diverted from his normal place of worship because of a snowstorm. In order to gain shelter he turned in to a Primitive Methodist Chapel. There were only about a dozen people there and the minister was not able to come because of the weather. Spurgeon writes:

> At last, a very thin-looking man . . . went up into the
> pulpit to preach. Now, it is well that preachers should be
> instructed, but this man was really stupid. He was
> obliged to stick to his text, for the simple reason that he
> had little else to say. The text was – 'Look unto me, and
> be ye saved, all the ends of the earth.'

Spurgeon then describes how the man very simply exhorted his congregation to look to Christ, briefly explaining that anybody could look, and that it was to Christ to whom they had to look.

> When he had managed to spin out about ten minutes or
> so, he was at the end of his tether. Then he looked at me
> in the gallery, and I daresay, with so few present, he
> knew me to be a stranger. Just fixing his eyes on me, as if
> he knew all my heart, he said, 'Young man, you look
> very miserable.' Well, I did, but I had not been
> accustomed to have remarks made from the pulpit on
> my personal appearance before. However, it was a good
> blow, struck right home. He continued, 'And you will
> always be miserable – miserable in life, and miserable in
> death – if you don't obey my text; but if you obey now,
> this moment, you will be saved.' Then, lifting up his
> hands, he shouted, as only a Primitive Methodist could
> do, 'Young man, look to Jesus Christ. Look! Look!
> Look! You have nothing to do but look and live.' I saw at
> once the way of salvation . . .[1]

The preacher was stronger on exhortation than on persuasive argument, but God nevertheless used this man to bring Spurgeon to faith. We should never lose sight of what God can do without skilful people. The basis for effectiveness is God and not human technique.

> *God can and does use unskilled people with no*
> *preparation, but his overruling of an*
> *unsatisfactory situation is no excuse for not*

*working for something good. The good is worth
aiming at. However, the good isn't everything.
The good without God is groundless.*

Two chestnuts

Should we bother about communication? Does the fact that
God *can* bypass normal routes mean that we should *not* be too
concerned with how we communicate? Sadly, some Christians would answer 'Yes' to the second question. At the risk
of over-simplification, those who would regard concern over
the quality of communication as pointless would probably fall
into one of two groups.

'God will tell me what to say'

Have you heard the one about the preacher who stood up and
announced that in his haste to arrive on time he'd left his
sermon notes at home? He was quite disconcerted when, on
hearing this, several members of the congregation exclaimed,
'Praise the Lord!'

When I first started preaching, I was horrified by the true
story of an old Methodist preacher who used to take a prayerful interest in me. Apparently, as a young man, he used to
visit a church where it was common practice for a steward to
give the preacher an envelope during the hymn before the
sermon. It wasn't the preacher's expenses, but the text he was
expected to preach on! The theory was that because the
preacher was given no time for 'human preparation', his
message would be bound to be more inspired. I suspect that
the church either closed fairly quickly or became full of
curious sadists.

I have met a few Christians who sadly feel that studying,
and concern about preparation, are somehow in conflict with
spirituality and effectiveness. There are at least four things
wrong with this position.

First, the biblical justification for it is very weak. Verses
such as Mark 13:11 are often quoted. In this verse Jesus tells
his disciples not to worry about what they are to say, for God

15

would tell them when the time came. However, the context is about times of persecution. It would be dubious exegesis to claim that just because God promises to miraculously help those who are dragged into difficult situations at short notice, he will also help unprepared speakers every time they stand up to communicate.

Secondly, those who argue that concern about technique is unspiritual hold a false view of inspiration. Why does the speaker have to wait until Sunday before inspiration comes? Can't God give it to him or her during the previous weeks of thought, reading, and prayer? Why is what has been thought about any less inspired than what has not been thought about? God rarely (if ever) bypasses the mind of the speaker. He frequently uses that mind. Many preachers will be able to tell of rare occasions when they felt compelled to change sections of their sermon or even the whole course of their message at the last moment because of clear promptings of the Holy Spirit. But those occasions are infrequent. The listeners are usually grateful for the hours of ordinary studying, praying, and thinking that God uses week by week.

Thirdly, surely technique can be inspired as well as content. In later chapters we shall be looking in detail at how particular speakers shaped their messages to help their hearers. Most good speakers are aware of at least two levels of preparation:

1. What is the content of my message?
2. How am I going to present the content in such a way that people will want to listen?

A common mistake of weak speakers is to be so concerned with content that they neglect presentation.

Whatever the reasons for neglect, it would be wrong to argue that concern over presentation is unspiritual. If metal-working and wood-carving can be Spirit-inspired (Exodus 31:1–11), then so can the craft of communicating.

Fourthly, in practice, such last-minute-inspired preachers often fail to convince the wider church of their inspiration. Their preaching is often anecdotal in the extreme and can be very self-centred as they relate numerous incidents that 'God has just brought to my mind'. More seriously, this kind of preaching never gets to grips with systematic, biblical exegesis. Consequently the preaching doesn't significantly contribute to the congregation's discipleship through the 'renewing of the mind' (Romans 12:2).

'It's all God's work anyway'

Some Christians, although they would share the church's concern over the biblical content of the message, would see the concern over technique as frivolous at best, and blasphemous at worst. They would stress God's role in making communication effective to the extent of denying man's responsibility in the process. They would argue that people understand Jesus because he opens their minds so they can understand the Scriptures (*cf.* Luke 24:27). And they will point to similar verses in Acts. Regardless of Paul's effectiveness as a speaker, Lydia was converted because 'the Lord opened her heart to respond to Paul's message' (Acts 16:14; *cf.* 13:48).

They extend their argument something like this:

> *God is all-powerful. He is in complete control of everything in the universe. Spiritual rebirth and growth depend on God moving in the life of the individual and on a miraculous awakening and understanding. If people fail to respond to a badly constructed and poorly presented message, it is because God has chosen not to work. The preacher cannot be held responsible. Books about communication represent a vain attempt to interfere with the sovereignty of God.*

Depending on your own theological persuasion you may agree with all or part of the above argument. But the problem for these Christians is that although the Bible clearly teaches the sovereignty of God, it also asks us to hold on to the seemingly irreconcilable position of human responsibility. God often chooses to work through the decisions and actions of responsible people. He holds them accountable for how they behave and evaluates the quality of their work.

There is certainly no apathy in Paul's desire to persuade people of the truth of the gospel. On the one hand Paul can rejoice in the sovereignty of God in salvation (Ephesians 1:3–5). On the other hand Paul modifies his behaviour so that his message is helped from a human point of view (1 Corinthians 9:19–23). The content of his sermon in Athens, and its style, are quite different from the sermon that he gives later in Jerusalem. (Compare Acts 17:16–31 with Acts 21:37 – 22:21.) He is constantly changing the presentation of his message to enhance his effectiveness. And nobody could accuse Paul of sitting back and resting on the sovereignty of God. Apart from the zeal of his missionary endeavours, the range of words used in Acts 17 and 18 to describe the variety and urgency of his communication is quite impressive. He reasoned, explained, proved, proclaimed, preached, persuaded, testified, taught, and vigorously refuted. There was nothing apathetic or indifferent about the content or the style of his preaching. Perhaps the outworking of the two seemingly irreconcilable beliefs in God's sovereignty and our responsibility in communication is seen most clearly in Paul's letter to the Colossians:

> We proclaim him, admonishing and teaching everyone
> with all wisdom, so that we may present everyone
> perfect in Christ. To this end I labour, struggling with
> all his energy, which so powerfully works in me
> (Colossians 1:28–29).

Paul knew that only God could do God's work, but he also knew that, in one sense, he had to act as if it all depended on him. Nevertheless, Paul is careful to acknowledge that all the ambition, energy, and drive to struggle for God's kingdom were inspired by God and not Paul.

> *Good presentation is worth aiming at, and*
> *although it isn't everything, we do have a*
> *responsibility to take it seriously.*

Some things to do

1. Meditate on 1 Timothy 4:11–16. What are the practical implications of these verses for you?

2. Get a notebook and jot down what you consider to be:
   - The similarities between preachers and salespersons.
   - The differences between preachers and salespersons.

CHAPTER 2

GOD'S EXAMPLE AS A COMMUNICATOR

It is sad that some people should use God's character as a reason for not taking communication more seriously. God is the communicator *par excellence*! In this chapter I want to take a look at God's determination to reach people, and his skill in doing so.

The Bible is full of examples of God using a variety of methods to get his message across. His communication testifies to great wisdom, imagination, and care. We know that the majesty of creation itself shouts out his glory and speaks to the world (Psalm 19:1–4). On a smaller scale God often used *visual aids and dramatic symbols* to reinforce his message and impress it on the minds of the hearers. He wanted them to understand and remember. Just imagine how powerfully the silent rainbow must have proclaimed God's grace to some of the immediate descendants of Noah. You can almost feel the nagging fears that many of them may have experienced every time there was a thunderstorm. Would God destroy them because of the sins of the previous week? But then what joy when they saw the rainbow!

At least once God *appealed to someone's natural curiosity* in order to gain a hearing, as when he used the burning bush to remind Moses of his holiness and power (Exodus 3:4). On other occasions he communicated in a much more subtle way. Clothes for priests were to be chosen with great care (Exodus 28:2). They were to serve as a constant reminder of the special status of the men who sacrificed on behalf of the people. The congregation were never to regard sin and sacrifice as 'ordinary'.

On many occasions God was not content to give general symbolic messages. He chose to speak to people, either directly or through his prophets. Sometimes he dropped in simple, but effective, *illustrations from everyday life* that helped the listener to understand and remember.

After a big battle and the denial of a great deal of money, God came to Abram with a message. He didn't give Abram an abstract theological treatise on the character of the Almighty. He simply reassured him with a personal statement involving a familiar object that Abram was unlikely to forget:

> 'Do not be afraid, Abram. I am your shield, your very
> great reward' (Genesis 15:1).

A few verses later on, as Abram stood under the night sky, God chose to reinforce his promise of children, again using something that a nomadic traveller would be constantly reminded of:

> 'Look up at the heavens and count the stars – if indeed
> you can count them.' Then he said to him, 'So shall
> your offspring be' (Genesis 15:5).

When he spoke to a rebellious, but now broken, nation, who wondered whether a fresh start was possible, he often used simple but powerful and enduring *imagery from nature and everyday life*:

> A bruised reed he will not break, and a smouldering
> wick he will not snuff out (Isaiah 42:3).

21

'I have swept away your offences like a cloud, your sins like the morning mist' (Isaiah 44:22).

Often God *asked questions*. He didn't do this because he wanted to know the answer (Psalm 94:9), but because he wanted to involve the audience in the learning process. By answering questions, listeners and readers would be drawn into understanding something important about themselves or about God (Genesis 3:9ff.; Haggai 2:10ff.). In this way he taught, not by declaring and hoping that the listeners would accept, but by leading them to a point where they themselves declared the truth that they would be unable to reject. By asking Adam and Eve questions God simply led them to acknowledge their own guilt. They could not argue with a divine accusation because they themselves had described their sin.

A similar method of getting a message across to stubborn listeners was to tell a 'simple' *story with a sting in the tail*. Listeners were invited to comment on some aspect of the action, and in so doing, condemned themselves with their own mouths. Every time I read the story of Jonah the determination of God to get through to the prophet never ceases to impress me. Apart from the skill and the irony of using the big fish to teach the reluctant fisher of men, the story of the vine in chapter 4 also reveals the care that God took to get his message across. Jonah is allowed to grow fond of a plant which provides a welcome shade after the successful and extensive preaching tour that Jonah didn't want to make. Then the plant is killed by a worm and Jonah is angry that something he cared for has been destroyed. At this point God uses Jonah's anger to reinforce his own message:

But God said to Jonah, 'Do you have a right to be angry about the vine?'

'I do,' he said. 'I am angry enough to die.'

But the Lord said, 'You have been concerned about this vine, though you did not tend it or make it grow. It sprang up overnight and died overnight. But Nineveh has more than a hundred and twenty thousand people who cannot tell their right hand from their left, and many cattle as well. Should I not be concerned about that great city?' (Jonah 4:9–11).

When seeking to reach the stubborn David after his adultery with Bathsheba and the murder of Uriah, God sends the prophet Nathan with an apparently harmless story about a rich man who stole another man's ewe lamb (2 Samuel 12). On hearing the story David burns with anger against the man and says to Nathan: 'As surely as the Lord lives, the man who did this deserves to die!'

It is not difficult to imagine the electrifying effect of Nathan's next words: 'You are the man!'

Sometimes when the speeches were long, and probably more difficult to listen to than the stories, or when he wished to achieve particular emphasis, God used simple *rhetorical devices* to regain attention: 'Hear, O Israel . . .', 'Remember this . . .', Be careful . . .', 'Be assured . . .', Understand then . . .' (Deuteronomy 9).

And have you noticed that the communication that God gave was always relevant? People either drank in his words because they met a particular heartfelt need, or they shrank from them as he put his finger on sensitive areas of their hearts. His hearers could never justly ask: 'What on earth has this got to do with me?' Unless they were incredibly hard, God was such a good communicator that they knew only too well what it had to do with them.

But there is more

I have dreadful trouble with the cars that I buy. When they refuse to start I often 'phone a friend who has a constant love affair with engines. I describe the symptoms: he tells me how to fix it. I describe what happens: he tells me what the next stage is. It's like one of those disaster films where the pilot of an aircraft has a heart attack and the plane is then flown by an untrained passenger who is talked through a near-perfect landing by an expert in the control tower. However, in my case we rarely make the landing. I don't seem to understand the instructions properly. I do the wrong thing. Usually, after half an hour my frustrated friend arrives in person to show me what to do. Seeing him at work, I understand in a fresh way.

God is so concerned with communication that not only does he speak in a variety of interesting and effective ways, he also comes himself so that people can see in reality and learn from the source. There is a certain sense in which Jesus is a 'walking sermon' – the 'Word made flesh'. But he is also a perfect model for Christian communicators. We should not only try to share his desire to reach people, and study the content of his message; we should also pay careful attention to his methodology.

In the light of what we know about God speaking in the Old Testament, it shouldn't surprise us that the communication of Jesus

- addresses specific and personal needs
- uses humour
- uses everyday illustrations
- questions and helps people to deduce truth for themselves
- gives structured messages
- uses language which is pithy and direct
- tells stories
- uses repetition for emphasis
- changes style and content according to his audience

Good communication is worth aiming at. In being concerned with communication we are seeking to be like God.

Some things to do

1. Suppose someone warned you against reading about the psychology of communication. Jot down three (or more) points that you would want to make in seeking to justify your interest in the communicator's craft.

2. Find two clean sheets in your notebook. At the top of one page write 'Good' and the the top of the other write 'Bad'. Quickly jot down on the appropriate page the characteristics of good and bad communication. Don't worry at this stage if you can't get too many points. You'll probably want to return to these pages at various stages in your reading. By the end of the book you should have at least fifteen points on each page. Find some friends to work at it with you and compare answers.

CHAPTER 3

ONE MAN AND HIS BOAT

So far I have tried to argue that the communicator's craft should be taken seriously. Now I want to raise your awareness of some general principles by asking you to think about what happens when communication fails. By establishing factors that contribute to failure we will be part way along the road to understanding success. I want you to reflect on a parable.

The outsider

The mountains were cypress-green and breathtakingly beautiful. Spiros was standing in one of the most impressive parts of Greece. On a brilliant spring morning he was standing at the foot of Mount Parnassus, a few miles from Corinth. In spite of the beauty, all he could think about was the problem of the boat which had rested in the sands of his mind for weeks now.

Should he buy it, or shouldn't he? If he didn't decide soon it would be too late. He had the money. Some had been left by his father; the rest had been painfully saved over the last ten years. But now, at the moment of decision, he seemed paralysed, unable to jump. It was such an important decision, such a lot of money, and he urgently needed a message from the gods. His wife had sent him to Delphi because her sister had been helped. Rumour and family superstition or experience had combined to encourage Spiros to think that the Delphic Oracle would make the divine will known.

And behind all this Spiros was driven by factors that were working at a less conscious level. Of course, he missed his father dreadfully, and at night, or alone in the harbour, suppressed questions surfaced.

Was there life beyond the grave?

Would he be good enough to please the gods?

Would he ever see his father again?

Were the gods really in control?

Perhaps the visit to the temple of Apollo would count for something. It might even provide a few answers.

Spiros felt his shyness acutely as he approached the temple. He tried to look serious and avoided eye contact with the others as he stood uneasily in the queue and waited for his turn to come. Perhaps he should have listened to his wife after all and worn the other clothes. This place seemed so strange and the glum faces of his fellow enquirers depressed him even more. He comforted himself with the fact that the embarrassment of leaving now and pushing past others to get out would be greater than the threat of staying. The ease of home was now as far away as the boat of his dreams.

Spiros knew that they would want his money (religious people usually did), but even so, the price that he had to pay for the sacrificial lamb still came as rather a shock. As he handed over the precious coins with poise and feigned devotion, he allowed himself to chuckle inwardly over the joke about the sinking ship. As it was going down in one of the storms off Crete, a desperate sailor had screamed out: 'Somebody do something religious. We're about to die!' And at that point another sailor picked up a plate and started taking a collection. Spiros now felt the bitterness of the joke more keenly than ever.

As the lamb was routinely disembowelled, Spiros noticed

the priest's indifference to the blood and gore. The religious man had seen it all before, many times. Spiros wasn't normally squeamish, but this spectacle offended his sensibilities and made him want to vomit. After briefly inspecting the carcass, the priest assured him that the omens were good. But Spiros had no intention of hanging around to ask questions, and nobody seemed willing to tell him. After all, the religious man had spoken, so who was Spiros to challenge the initiated?

A man in drab clothes with a hard face took more money and then put Spiros' request on to a lead tablet. Again there was more ceremony that Spiros didn't understand before he was eventually ushered into the inner temple and mystery. At last! The route to possible understanding had been long, embarrassing, and costly (not least for the lamb).

A few yards in front of him a priestess, in ritual garments, was sitting on a stool near a chasm in the rock. She ignored his presence and this apparent aloofness made Spiros feel both angry and afraid. Was she mad? It certainly looked as if she was out of control. He remembered that his sister-in-law had said something about a woman fainting. The fumes from the chasm were obviously important to the ceremony. The priestess inhaled them eagerly and mumbled incomprehensibly. So this was it, thought Spiros, the heart of the religious experience.

He strained forward to catch her words. It was no good. He would never remember what she was saying, and it made no sense anyway. Religious mumbo-jumbo? A foreign language? How was he to know?

Spiros could feel his contempt rising, although he was afraid to show anger in the presence of Apollo. How could he make sense of all this? As he looked around seeking scraps of information, and an escape, he noticed a scribe writing frantically. Perhaps the scribe knew the language. A few more scribbles and contortions of the face (obviously reflecting inspiration) and then the man looked at Spiros (or rather, through him), and spoke:

'One of the signs of the growing of truth is the clouds in the heavens. Look to the winds for the direction of life and the shifting of treasure.'

Years later, a learned friend of his would tell Spiros that he had been taken in by the subconscious effects of the poetry. At the time Spiros had just been thrilled to hear something in his own language, even if it did sound rather vague and archaic. For a few extra coins it was written down and Spiros left with his answer. At least somebody had communicated what Apollo had said. His need had been met.

It was obvious to Spiros that Apollo was telling him to buy the boat. He would make his fortune by using the wind to fill its sails.

Three-and-a-half years later, as he started a life sentence for debt, Spiros began to wonder if he had misunderstood what Apollo had said. And the suppressed questions about death still nagged. Perhaps he would now have more time to think seriously about them.

Some things to do

1. Using the parable as a starting point, discuss or jot down the factors which contribute to communication failure. You may find it helpful to think of factors under the following headings: Message, Speaker, Delivery, Hearer, Environment, Other Factors.

2. Imagine that a nineteen-year-old, poorly educated, unemployed male, who has never been to church in his life before, turned up at one of your church services by mistake.
   - What things would make him feel uneasy?
   - What things wouldn't he have much chance of understanding?
   - How could all those things be changed to improve the situation?

CHAPTER 4

THE NEED FOR STRUCTURE

Overview

Why is it necessary to think carefully about the structure of the messages that you want to give? Why not just present the thoughts as they occur to you? Surely this would be more natural?

This chapter

- looks at how structure helps people to understand and remember messages
- explains why structure is particularly important for helping spoken messages
- suggests one way of 'building on' to an already existing framework

Chapter 5 briefly considers five common ways of ordering material.

Just suppose

Just suppose that it is Christmas Eve. You are a weary student who has taken a temporary vacation job in a large Post Office, in order to earn enough cash to keep yourself in books and biscuits for next term. The novelty of trudging through slush in near freezing weather wore off a week ago. It's about an hour before your shift ends and you have come back to the office to help repair parcels before regaining your freedom. Sitting at a table with string, tape, and an over-zealous first-year philosophy student, you are discussing the logical grounds for believing that you exist.

Suddenly you are told to help process a consignment of parcels that has appeared. These have to be sorted quickly in time for the special delivery that is going out that evening.

You find yourself in a large room containing a mountain of parcels, a terrifying array of trolleys, and a small number of people who appear to know what they are doing. The parcels that come to you at one end of the room have to be put in the correct containers on the trolleys at the other end of the room. There's obviously a system for working out how to put the parcels in the right containers with speed, but as your shift ends, you realize that in the short time available, you never really understood what it was. You leave for home feeling slightly discouraged.

And as you sit in your cold and rusty car in the Christmas Eve traffic jam, you wish that the sorting could have been done before the parcels actually reached your hands. It would have made your job much less stressful. Instead of facing parcels coming at random, you wanted them to come in small batches which were already sorted. You wanted someone to say:

'The next four go in container H.'

'The next eighteen go in container A.'

'The next seven . . .'

Structure and sense

Words are like parcels – packages of information. When listening to somebody speaking, or when reading a book, your brain is trying to make sense of the thousands of words that pour into the ears or through the eyes. Under certain conditions the brain can process these words at an incredible pace. A fluent reader can read well-written material at about 300 words a minute (or five words a second). The preferred rate for both silent reading and listening to spoken language for many people is approximately three words a second.[1] Even this slower rate is still impressively fast.

One of the keys to helping understanding and to making the listening or reading process less stressful, is to make sure that the words are clearly sorted *before* they are given to other people to understand. You find it easier to read a chapter or listen to a sermon that has clearly labelled sections, or ways of saying to you:

'These words are about subject X.'

'When you've processed these, the next batch of words is going to be about subject Y.'

'By the way, I've just finished giving you the words about X, so you can switch to Y now.'

The mind is being warned about what to expect and can prepare appropriate containers for the packages.

The person who tries to understand what somebody is communicating is like a detective trying to solve a crime. Having clues (words) is not enough. What detectives need to do is to relate clues to other clues and to an overall picture. They need to be able to impose structured patterns on apparent chaos. Similarly the reader and the listener need to be able both to link words together, and to be able to see the significance of particular sentences against an overall framework. Until they can do that, understanding will be minimal. Clearly structured messages help the reader and the listener to make those links.

Structure and memory

Structured messages are not only easier to understand, they are also more memorable. You can talk about the three or four main points of a clearly structured sermon over Sunday lunch, but poorly structured ramblings are usually lost by the end of the service.

In one sense this is obvious. Imagine that the structure was removed from the language you are reading. Just suppose that the words no longer conformed to patterns of grammatical structure and rearranged themselves within sentences. And then imagine the sentences becoming rearranged within paragraphs, and paragraphs within chapters, and chapters within the book. The result would be a meaningless mass of thousands of words. It's certain that nobody would be able to understand the message, let alone remember it.

Psychologists and educationalists such as D. P. Ausubel, V. M. Cashen, K. L. Leicht and J. Dooling have conducted various experiments to assess the importance of structure in helping understanding and memory.[2] Students of various ages and abilities were asked to read different types of passages and then answer questions about what they had read.

Some passages had all structural support removed. Paragraph divisions were removed and features such as headings, sub-headings, and sentences at the beginning summarizing the content of the passage or paragraph were left out. These were precisely the features which would help the reader make sense of and remember the words. These features have been labelled 'advance organizers' because they give advance warning to the brain about how to organize the incoming data.

In other passages paragraph divisions were left intact and advance organizers were included. In some studies the latter were highlighted by being printed in bold letters or by being underlined.

What researchers found was that when they tested readers on what they could remember from the passages, the passages which had the advance organizers produced significantly higher scores. And it wasn't just that people could remember the highlighted material better. The structural support given by the advance organizers actually helped readers to understand and remember the rest of the material. Having remembered the main elements and key ideas, the readers could then reconstruct the details of the passages.

Of course, unless you were an actor who had learned the

script, you would not be able to remember all the exact words of any passage you had read or of any talk you had listened to. What you actually remember is the gist of what was communicated. The gist is simply a summary of the main ideas, which in turn corresponds very closely to any advance organizers given in the passage. And by remembering the gist of a clearly structured passage, you would almost certainly be able to reconstruct much of the rest of the message. A friend of mine recently told me that she could remember the main points of a sermon on Hannah. Alliteration and a clear structure helped the listener remember that the speaker talked of Hannah as being a woman in pain, a woman in prayer, and a woman in praise. These points provided a key for releasing other memories and for reconstructing other parts of the message.

> *Language and ideas that are carefully organized*
> *are much more likely to be understood and*
> *remembered than poorly structured material.*

Differences between reading and listening

Often the mind faces considerable pressure to process large amounts of information quickly. This pressure is most acute when listening to a talk, and especially to a talk where the speaker has no visual aids or hand-outs (*i.e.* most sermons).

Readers can control the flow of information by putting the book down. They can give themselves time to clear the backlog of parcels by pausing for thought, by re-reading difficult passages, and by asking for help.

However, when listening to a talk, the listener usually can't stop the speaker or rewind what has been said in order to relisten to it. And uncertainties can't be clarified until later. The words usually just keep on coming. The listener can get round the processing problem by thinking about Sunday lunch, but this means that understanding is lost.

The reason listeners face a more difficult task than readers is that speech exists only in *time*, whereas the printed page exists both in *space and time*. Because of this, a person delivering a sermon faces a very different task from someone writing the same message for a religious magazine.

As has been mentioned above, writers have several options for indicating the structure of their messages so that the reader can see how the words have been sorted. But speakers do not have such a permanent way of indicating the structure. Any structural clues that are given exist in time for a second. And whereas the writer can use subtle devices that the reader can study at leisure, the speaker has to rely more on the words themselves.

Words which signal the relationships of one statement to another are important in indicating structure and are particularly important in speech.

Cause/effect	*because, since, therefore, consequently, as a result, nevertheless, accordingly, if . . . then.*
Comparison/contrast	*however, but, as well as, on the other hand, not only . . . but also, either . . . or, while, although, unless, similarly, yet.*
Time order	*on (date), not long after, now, as, before, when.*
Simple listing	*to begin with, first, second, next, then, finally.*

Pauses and differences of tone, of volume, of tempo have to be combined with words to attempt to achieve for a brief moment what the writer can achieve for history on the page.

> *All communication needs to be structured, but structure is even more important in speech than in writing. The listener can't 're-read the page'. Structure is vital if he or she is to remember what you said.*

Linking up to the listener

Advance organizers can also be used to perform a slightly different function. In addition to giving information about structure, they can link into the receivers' background in other ways. 'You already know about X, Y, Z. Well, what I am going to introduce to you today is very similar to what you already know (or perhaps contrasts with what you already know). Think about X, Y, Z and it will help you understand the new material.' Advance organizers can be used to identify areas of understanding that the audience *already has* so that new material can be attached to it. Like using illustrations, it goes back to the idea of finding hooks in the minds of people on to which you can hang your coat. As you use advance organizers in this way you are reminding people to get out particular hooks ready for the coat you are about to hand over to them.

In my experience this type of advance organizer has two particularly useful functions. When delivering a series of sermons to the same congregation you often want to remind people of what you have said before. Some speakers overdo it and end up preaching the same sermon all over again. Others skilfully summarize the material and leave it at that. On occasions a better way of doing it would be to use the material as an advance organizer and say: 'You already know this material. What I'm going to introduce to you relates to it in this way.'

> We spent some time last week reminding ourselves of Jesus' warning that the Devil is a liar and we started to consider what this warning meant in one specific area. We are sometimes taken in by his lies about evangelism. You'll remember that one lie we often believe is that evangelism doesn't matter, and I tried to show you why this belief is wrong.
>
> What I want to do this week is to take the subject further by looking at other lies we believe about evangelism. Last week we were thinking about evangelism in general. This week I want us to think in particular about the lies dealing with our own

ability to engage in evangelism. We so often fail to take evangelism seriously because we believe the lie: 'I can't tell people about my faith. That kind of activity is only for the super-spiritual or the super-gifted.' We've already thought about how God declares that evangelism is important. Now we are going to look at why all of us have a responsibility to evangelize and how he can give us the grace to do so.

A second particularly useful function that this type of organizer can have is in emphasizing the distinctiveness of Christian teaching in contrast to something else. In the organizer you set out what views are commonly held and then explain that you are gong to argue that the Bible teaches something different. In this way you bring into consciousness what people already know as well as setting out the overall plan for your message.

Some people think that 'love' means having nice feelings towards those people who have nice feelings towards them, but that is not what Jesus meant when he commanded us to love one another as he had loved us. He was talking about a kind of love that went far beyond feelings. He was talking about a kind of love that involved both the mind and will and which is far greater than ordinary, or even good, friendship. It's this kind of love that I want us to consider this morning.

The beginning of any message can be crucial in helping to determine whether or not it will be received with any degree of understanding. Advance organizers can be used to relate the message to what the audience already knows as well as to give structural information.

Some things to do

1. Get some friends to listen to you giving a talk (but don't tell them why you want them to listen). About an hour

37

after you have finished your talk, ask them if they understood and can remember the structure of your message.

2. Listen to yourself on tape. Pay close attention to the key words on pp. 35. Do you think that you clearly indicate the relationship between your ideas?

3. Look over a talk that you have given recently and write an advance organizer for the material. Get a friend to help you evaluate its effectiveness in helping to improve comprehension and motivate your audience to listen to your message.

DIFFERENT TYPES OF STRUCTURE

There are as many ways of structuring communication as there are people. Any good talk or piece of writing will probably include a variety of sub-structures within an overall plan.

Forgive me if it seems obvious, but in order to deliver a well structured message, you need to know what points you want to make. After listening to some speakers you may be forgiven for wondering if *they* knew what they were trying to say. Bad communication is like trying to conduct sophisticated surgery using a failing fluorescent tube – the light lacks focus. Tens of thousands of religious or moral words do not necessarily act as a blazing light to expose darkness.

Before delivering a message I try to make sure that I can answer two questions:

1. What are the *main points* I expect my congregation to have learnt after listening to me for nearly half an hour?
2. What *precisely* do I want them to *do* as a result of listening to me?

Until I can answer these questions I have no idea of what I

want to say or achieve. Unless I can answer these questions my attempts at structuring will be like building a wall with straw.

What I want to do in this chapter is to outline five popular frameworks for structuring material.

The list structure

Introduction

1. Fact or argument

2. Fact or argument

3. Fact or argument

4. Fact or argument

This type of overall plan is quite common. It is suitable for talks where you want to convey a lot of material, but where the points aren't necessarily related to each other in any clear, logical sequence – where you're not necessarily trying to lead people to a particular conclusion.

I was recently asked to give a twenty-minute lunch-time talk on the Book of Proverbs. What I wanted to do in the limited time available was to give some basic information about the book and some brief illustrative examples of some of its teaching. The implicit aim of the talk was to encourage my listeners to study the book, but there wasn't time available to extend this point at any length. The structure of the talk was therefore not directly leading to any developed conclusion, but was merely a framework for imparting information.

I structured the ideas in the following way:

Very brief introduction to encourage listening.

1. The book is a *textbook* on how to live wisely. It has several characteristic features of textbooks:
   a. Repetition of key ideas.

     b.   Use of everyday objects to teach points.
     c.   Use of questions and riddles to involve the reader.
     d.   Vivid and sometimes shocking comparisons to help in making the teaching memorable.

2. Helpful things to remember when studying the book:
     a.   It makes statements about what generally happens and not promises about what will inevitably happen in every case.
     b.   It should be approached like a database and not like a story-book.

3. Summary of contents – fear God.

4. Why is it relevant today? A summary of its teaching on relationships.

None of the main points mentioned above is closely related in any logical sense to any of the others. This can be easily demonstrated by the fact that, once the introduction has been given, the order of the main points could be shuffled around without dramatically affecting the effectiveness of the talk.

Part of my work involves me in reading thousands of words produced by relatively intelligent young adults. On some occasions, after having read hundreds of words, I find myself writing comments such as the following:

> *I liked the particular point you made on page 3 about X, but we need to discuss your overall structure. Please show me the list of points you intended to convey. At times I found myself struggling to follow the argument and to answer the question: 'What are her main points?'*

Lists may be one of the simplest forms of structure, but note that the very fact of writing down the points you wish to convey forces you to impose some form of order on the initial random collection of thoughts. Without the discipline of a list your speaking or writing will wander. Vague writing faces the blue pencil of an editor. Congregations are less brutal, and many endure hours of talks that go round the universe in order to get nowhere. If you can't list the points you want to get across, you don't really know what you want to say, and your hearers certainly won't learn what it is.

The lead-on structure

Introduction

1. Fact or argument

2. Fact or argument

3. Fact or argument

Conclusion

This kind of general structure is quite suitable for sermons because it is designed to lead to conclusions that are difficult to ignore. In effect it is saying: 'In the light of all these things, *this* is what we ought to believe and how we ought to live.' In Christian communication we are usually speaking or writing in order to change lives and not merely to inform. The purpose of the lead-on is to make it difficult for people to fail to reach the conclusion that we want them to reach. The lead-on isn't meant just to scatter our seeds: it's meant to bury them in hearts.

I tend to use the simple lead-on structure most often when I am giving evangelistic talks. We need to think through objections that people have to Christianity and be prepared to argue our case. Having presented the arguments and facts clearly, there is then a natural follow-on to the conclusions we want people to reach and actions that we want them to take.

I have listed below the structure of a talk that I gave at an evangelistic meal on the title 'Who is Jesus? And does it matter anyway?' I do not claim originality for the material. Those who have benefited from the reading and clear reasoning of C. S. Lewis, Josh McDowell or Stephen Gaukroger will recognize my sources.

Very brief introduction to encourage listening.

Argument 1: Jesus existed in history. He wasn't a fictional character. Quote early historians.

Argument 2: It doesn't make sense to argue that Jesus was a bad man who tricked people. His enemies couldn't find fault in him. Why be tortured to death for a lie?

Argument 3: It doesn't make sense to argue that he was a mad man. His character, his teaching, his relationships all testify to his sanity.

Argument 4: It isn't good enough to say that Jesus was simply a good man. Good men don't do what Jesus did. Jesus claimed to be God. Jesus rose from the dead.

↓

Because Jesus is God, he has a right to your love and obedience.

↓

This is how you start to follow him.

In the list structure the speaker is showing the listeners separate piles of knowledge bricks, which they may or may not choose to take away and use in their own building. In the lead-on structure, the speaker is building a house in front of the listeners and then inviting them in to stay.

The process of building is important for at least two reasons. First, an element of suspense is involved. The listeners are naturally curious to see how the building is going to turn out. This structure tends to keep people guessing as they try to solve the riddle of what your conclusions are going to be, and they tend to be more involved because of this. Secondly, if you build carefully, people will assess the quality of your argument and will have more confidence in entering the final building than they would have done if you had simply said, 'This is the building. Come in!' Where you have a potentially indifferent or hostile audience whose views you wish to change (*i.e.* in most evangelistic situations), the lead-on structure helps to get you a hearing.

The justification structure

Introduction

Statement of belief or thesis

↓

1. Fact or argument

2. Fact or argument

3. Fact or argument

Summary/Restatement of belief or thesis

↓

Possible courses of action

In the lead-on structure the speaker carefully builds the house from the ground. In the justification structure the speaker starts by showing the house that has already been built and then explains to the audience why it was built in the way that it was.

The justification structure suits the kind of talk where you want to explain something new or slightly controversial to a *sympathetic* audience. The focus of this structure tends to be on *why* you believe what you believe, rather than the belief itself.

I was once asked by a church to explain my understanding of what the Bible teaches about baptism and I knew that my own views differed from the views of some of the congregation. I started by stating what my position was. There was no point in trying to use suspense to keep people guessing till later on in the talk. I had spoken openly about my views with the people who invited me to preach. But having stated my position, I then had to justify my beliefs through biblical exegesis. For the listeners, what was new and potentially helpful was not the thesis itself, but the biblical justification behind it.

The contrast structure

Introduction

1*a*.   Some people say/do this . . .
1*b*.   *But* I say/do this . . .

2*a*.   Some people say/do this . . .
2*b*.   *But* I say/do this . . .

3*a*.   Some people say/do this . . .
3*b*.   *But* I say/do this . . .

General conclusions. Suggestions for action if these have not already been covered in 1–3.

Making a point by contrasting what somebody else has said with what you want to say is quite a common way of highlighting the importance and apparent wisdom of your own material. Politicians frequently introduce their own policies by describing the failures of the policies of their opponents first. But beware. It is not good enough to criticize what people may be already thinking and doing. You have to be able to offer something better to replace it. Unless you can offer a better alternative they will resent your criticism.

The contrast structure has several advantages. First, by

demonstrating to people the inadequacy of what somebody else would have them believe, they are more disposed to take your own suggestions in a positive light. If you take the carpet from underneath people's feet they will feel uneasy, and will be more likely to step onto any new carpet that you can provide.

Secondly, by taking genuine words and actions of others as your starting point, you are doing two things which are a common factor in much successful communication: you are starting where people are with issues that are relevant to them, and are starting with something concrete. Look at how Jesus used this technique to great effect in the Sermon on the Mount. He frequently uses the following structure:

> *You have heard it said . . . But I tell you . . .*[1]

In Matthew 6 Jesus describes the actions of the hypocrites in great detail before going on to emphasize his own teaching on prayer and fasting. He was taking words about practical issues that his audience would have understood. Having got them to recognize the teaching and practices, he then proceeds to develop his own views.

I have listed below the structure of a sermon based on Colossians 3:13, 'Forgive as the Lord forgave you'. I wanted to convey the idea that Christian forgiveness has to be something more than the kind of forgiveness that is practised by the average non-Christian.

Introduction to encourage listening and relate the topic of forgiveness to the needs of the hearers.

Brief background to the epistle explaining why forgiveness was an issue for the Colossian church. Onesimus had been sent back to Philemon by Paul, and the Colossian church met in Philemon's house.

1*a*. Non-Christian forgiveness is often reluctantly given.

1*b*.   Christ forgives freely and therefore Christians should do the same.

2*a*.   Non-Christian forgiveness can be proud and condescending.

2*b*.   Christians should forgive with humility.

3*a*.   Non-Christians often set limits on what they will forgive.

3*b*.   Christ says that only the sin against the Holy Spirit will not be forgiven.
   Christians should not therefore have long lists of unforgivable sins with which to condemn themselves and others.

4*a*.   Non-Christians often want a price to be paid before they will forgive. Such forgiveness is conditional on a list of requirements. 'I'll forgive her if . . .'

4*b*.   Christ has paid the price, therefore Christian forgiveness should not expect people to pay a price before being forgiven. The only 'condition' is repentance.

↓

Conclusion. We should seek to be reconciled to God and to each other.

↓

Practical suggestions for action.

   A common variation of the contrast structure given above is to save the contrast until the second part of the message, rather than make it with every point.

Introduction

I'm going to talk about SUBJECT.

47

1. By SUBJECT I *don't mean* X.

2. By SUBJECT I *don't mean* Y.

3. By SUBJECT I *don't mean* Z.

4. But I *do* mean A.

5. I *do* mean B.

6. I *do* mean C.

I can remember hearing a sermon by Dr Lawrence Crabb on the subject of 'intimacy'. In the first part of the sermon Dr Crabb systematically stripped away preconceptions that people may have had about the subject before he expounded what he believed the Bible taught. I can remember that by the second part of the sermon I was desperate to know what he did mean by 'intimacy' because all the views that I would have argued at the time had been shown to be inadequate. Suspense (and therefore a greater listener involvement) is the main advantage of this particular variation.

The story structure

Of all the structures listed in this chapter, stories are perhaps the easiest to remember. We may not feel too much at home in the realm of logical argument, but all of us have been listening to stories for as long as we can remember. All of us understand something of their conventions, and once one has started, we find it difficult not to listen to the conclusion.

There are three common elements in most stories:

1. *Setting*. The physical/social climate in which the story takes place. The who-where-when information.

2. *Conflict*. In order to have a story there must be some sort of disruption to the normal routine

that causes conflict between characters, or internal conflict within characters.

3. *Resolution of conflict.* The interest in the story lies in following (and perhaps guessing) how the character(s) will resolve the situation that arose in 2.

In Christian communication one of the major roles served by stories is their use as an illustration of or basis for particular points of teaching. In Acts 7 the overall structure of Stephen's sermon is the lead-on, the conclusion of which is Acts 7:51–53. His conclusion is not preceded by a series of logical arguments, however, but by a mass of historical sketches (stories from history).

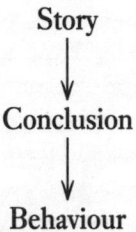

Story

↓

Conclusion

↓

Behaviour

Whether we are telling fictional stories about seven-year-olds to illustrate the key concept of a children's talk, or illustrating a sermon by telling the true story of a pilot who sacrificed his life to save the lives of hundreds, we are using this structure as a form of compelling argument that people will understand.

Combined structures

In practice, most communication will use a mixture of structures to impose some sort of order on words and thus to help shape and fine-tune the meaning. We state a thesis and then justify it by reasoning and a story. We precede a conclusion with both a story and an argument (and part of that argument may include a

49

series of contrasts). Again, the Sermon on the Mount is a good example of this. It is at least arguable that the Sermon contains list, contrast and story structures. The key issue is that we should help people to process the vast amounts of language that we give to them by carefully arranging the way in which the parcels are presented.

Some things to do

1. Think through the advantages and disadvantages of each of the five structures outlined above. Try to think of an occasion, a topic, and an audience that would be appropriate for each one.

2. Look through a talk you have given and try to note its structure. Experiment with the material by adapting and rearranging it to make it fit at least two other structures. Does this improve the original talk, and if so, why?

3. What is the structure of the Sermon on the Mount?

CHAPTER 6

BRIDGING GAPS: EXAMPLES

Overview

Unfortunately, a well constructed message will not necessarily succeed in attracting a hearing. We've all heard erudite but totally incomprehensible or boring speakers. As we saw towards the end of Chapter 4, when we were looking at advance organizers, the message has to relate to what the listener already knows if it is to be understood. This chapter emphasizes the importance of linking the message to the receiver's background and suggests how we can use *examples* in order to go about it.

People use what they already know

What can you remember about the last wedding you went to?

Some years ago a team of psychologists[1] asked two groups of people to read accounts of two weddings. One group of readers was a sample of American students; the other group were Indian students. Several hours after the reading they were asked to write down what they could remember about the passages. It was extremely interesting to see quite important differences between the two groups of memories. Each group had clearly interpreted the passages in the light of its own cultural norms. The Americans remembered most about the bride and the elaborate ritual involved, whereas the Indians remembered most about the social status of the families and concentrated more on the importance of the men.

What this study helped to confirm was that we use what is already in our minds to interpret incoming information. The best communicators are those who are able to understand the kinds of experience and knowledge that we already have. They are then able to forge links between what we already know and what they want us to know.

> *Successful communicators use examples that make*
> *sense to the listener so that the new material is less*
> *threatening and puzzling. Illustrations are a*
> *bridge into the receiver's brain. The communicator*
> *can use them to carry new understanding. As*
> *Spurgeon said: 'Illustrations are like windows —*
> *they let in light.'*

Give us an example

Don't punch people with a raw idea: shake their hands with an example.

I was recently quite shocked when two people from the same church, on separate occasions, actually quoted to me parts of messages that I had delivered months previously. Before you think that I am on some kind of ego trip, let me put their words into perspective. On the first occasion the person had genuinely forgotten that I was the speaker. He had almost certainly forgotten the subject of the talk and at least 80% of what had been said. On the second occasion the speaker was actually trying to encourage me, not by the fact that he could remember what I had said, but by quoting my own words to dispel my own lack of faith. The crucial point, however, is that on both occasions what was quoted back to me was not some heavy theological argument or profound quotation, but two very simple illustrations that I had used.

Very often the things which are remembered most are the illustrations. Because they are concrete and often personal, they are a very good way of encapsulating abstract truth. We *could* get the same truth across without them, but both speakers/writers and listeners/readers would have to work much harder in order to achieve less success. Jesus, after all, was a master at conveying his message through stories and vivid pictures.

Sources of examples

Good examples are worth thousands of words. Although years ago I would have rejected the suggestion out of hand, it now seems to me so obvious that any communicator concerned about improving his or her craft needs to collect examples systematically. If I see a good example, I have to record it. Like a squirrel, I need to gather and hoard material while it is available, so that when winter comes my cupboard isn't bare.

I used to tell myself that I would remember the examples that I had read or heard. But I lost hundreds that way because I could never remember them when I wanted them. Now I always have a pencil with me when I read so that I can jot down illustrations at the time of reading. When I've finished a book or article, I record the examples on cards and store them alphabetically in index boxes under topics. I list the gist of the story or idea, the author, and the page number and title of the book if appropriate. This last piece of information is useful when I find that the notes I made about an example don't make much sense five years after they were originally written down. I can check details against the source.

Such a procedure may seem unnecessarily cumbersome to some people. I would argue that we store what is important to us, and for me, good examples are too valuable an aid to communication to waste.

Of course, we will frequently need to invent our own examples. Let's think creatively with the minds given us by the creator God and try to invent interesting and helpful illustrations to communicate his truth. I can think of six possible sources of illustrations.

Example source 1: films, videos, television, and books

I know of one evangelist who tries to go to the cinema fairly regularly just to find out what some of his hearers will have been watching, and to find examples from these films to illustrate his talks. I'm not for a moment arguing that we shouldn't enjoy certain aspects of the cinema for its own sake, but because television and films are very powerful media and are watched and discussed daily by millions, they are useful bridges into people's understanding.

I can remember one speaker starting an evangelistic talk by discussing the screen death that week of a pet dog on a very popular daily soap opera, and how the attitude of the characters in the series to the death raised all sorts of questions about life beyond the grave. Immediately many of his audience understood what he was talking about and warmed to his subject. He would have had a much harder time if he had announced: 'This evening I want to consider the subject of the resurrection.'

Paul showed on several occasions that his reading hadn't been entirely limited to the Old Testament (Acts 17:28; 1 Corinthians 10:7; 2 Timothy 3:8; Titus 1:12). His ability to quote Greek poetry (Acts 17:28; Titus 1:12) enabled him to disarm his critics. He made his point by using sources that his audience were likely to agree with. The writing and preaching of communicators such as Billy Graham, Josh McDowell, Michael Green, and Os Guinness carry authority partly because they are so well informed about what modern man is thinking. They are able to draw from their extensive reading of modern writing to illustrate their messages.

Example source 2: real events

If we describe the details well we will find people drawn into the account because of natural curiosity. And examples taken from life often have great force because they are about real people. What we are often saying is, 'These people tried and failed, therefore listen carefully to this point,' or, 'These people tried and succeeded, therefore be encouraged by their example. They were only ordinary people like you and me.' Corrie ten Boom, describing her feelings after the Second World War when she met the prison camp officer who had hurt her sister, provides a far greater example of forgiveness than I could ever hope to invent. And listeners are able to recognize the weight of the authentic example which captures the pains and joys of being a Christian in the real world.

In a society that didn't have newspapers or television, history was an important source of information for a society's shared knowledge. In the Bible speakers are often quoting events from national history as examples of God's great love and of the failure of people.

As well as using real events as factual examples of particular truths, they can also serve as parables or symbols for spiritual truth. Jesus often did this. In John 9, for example, we find him talking to Pharisees about spiritual blindness and judgment. But the spiritual truth of what he is saying has been well illustrated by the real events preceding his statement. The Pharisees have refused to accept that a blind man has been healed by Jesus.

The real events of the feeding of the crowds in John 6 become a powerful metaphor for the sufficiency of Christ as the Bread of Life. This doesn't mean that the feeding of the crowds is unimportant in itself. It clearly is. But because a real, dramatic event is embedded in the people's minds, Jesus uses it as a convenient vehicle for 'greater' spiritual truth.

Some speakers keep newspaper cuttings of stories they can use as illustrations. I've also seen various natural disasters that were dominating television news used to illustrate some aspect of Christian truth. Because pictures from the television are fresh in the listeners' minds, the messages seem to have a poignancy and power. (For example, 'Just as the rescuer risked his own life and climbed into the unstable building to bring out the child, so too Christ . . .') I'm not arguing that we should fail to see the serious issues behind the news because of our search for sermon fodder. I'm simply suggesting that we should be more aware of the rich sources of bridges into people's minds.

Example source 3: the natural world

I once worked in a school where the staff and pupils used to groan inwardly and suppress sniggers two or three times a year when the head teacher gave the same assembly. He was always telling us about the ant from the book of Proverbs (Proverbs 6:6). But did you know about the lion in the book of Proverbs (Proverbs 22:13) or about the pig with the ring in its nose (Proverbs 11:22)? I've already mentioned how God used a plant to teach Jonah a lesson. On another occasion he compared the nation of Israel unfavourably to a disobedient ox or donkey (Isaiah 1:3). Jesus often used the natural world to reinforce his points. Some of his most famous words use lilies, grass, and sparrows to teach about abstract concepts such as faith and discipleship (Matthew 6:28–34). Fortunately, God's creation is so rich in variety we are unlikely to run out of creatures and plants with which to compare human beings and from which to draw important lessons.

Undoubtedly the most successful examples from the natural world are those which people can easily understand. Listeners in biblical times could more immediately recognize the points of some comparisons than perhaps we can. Few of us have the knowledge gained from working daily with animals that many of the biblical listeners would have had. It is perfectly possible to use the hibernating patterns of a particular species of desert toad to illustrated a point about spiritual lethargy. However, you would have to do an awful lot of explaining first to fill in the background details for most congregations in Western societies.

Example source 4: the family

How many children have 'suffered' from being born into the homes of preachers or writers and from being continually used as illustrative material? Although you obviously need to be sensitive when talking about your grandparents, grandchildren, children, spouse, or mother-in-law, the actions and sayings of your family are usually things which other ordinary people can understand and identify with. And because God describes himself in the Bible as both mother and father (Isaiah 49:13–15; Psalm 103:13), the parent–child relationship is often a rich source of examples. (Even where individuals have a poor image of motherhood and fatherhood, such examples can be used to teach spiritual truth through contrasting people's present experience with what God reveals.)

One of my own earliest memories of trying to come to grips with what faith is centres on a story told by a preacher about his daughter clutching her father's hand as they crossed a busy road. I began to see that faith meant trust based on an understanding of God's character. Jesus was certainly able to use the parent–child relationship to illustrate theological truth:

> 'Which of you fathers, if your son asks for a fish, will give him a snake instead? Or if he asks for an egg, will give him a scorpion? If you then, though you are evil, know how to give good gifts to your children, how much more will your Father in heaven give the Holy Spirit to those who ask him!' (Luke 11:11–13).

Example source 5: the world of work

Like the family, the world of work is an area of life that large numbers of people can identify with. Although each congregation is likely to contain some unemployed people, most have, or have had, regular employment.

Look at the range of occupations that Jesus covers in his examples. On one occasion Jesus was able to appeal to the experience that many people would have had in the building industry to illustrate the need to evaluate the cost of becoming a disciple (Luke 14:28–30). On another occasion he shows that he is not unsympathetic to some of the problems faced by employers and middle managers (Luke 16:1–12).

And Jesus frequently draws examples from farming, fishing, and shepherding (perhaps three of the most common sources of employment in his day) to illustrate the kingdom of God (Matthew 13:1–30, 47–52; Luke 15:1–7). Jesus was also very careful not to exclude women. In an age when most women worked at home, he included their work experience as a source of illustration (Luke 15:8–10).

Example source 6: objects

You may have heard of the Alan Bennett sketch in which the clergyman describes undoing a sardine tin, and then says the immortal words: 'And you know, life is just like that ...' When taken to such extremes this kind of example can be absurd and strained. You can always recognize the speaker who has been asked to give too many children's talks to the same congregation: he or she runs round the house picking up objects and mumbling: 'Now, what can I use this to illustrate?' What spiritual truth could *you* teach with a yo-yo or a broken hair-grip?

In spite of the possibility of abuse, and of awkward comparisons, objects can provide very useful illustrations. Jesus had sufficient confidence in the method to teach an effective lesson to a hostile audience:

> He saw through their duplicity and said to them, 'Show me a denarius. Whose portrait and inscription are on it?'
> 'Caesar's,' they replied.
> He said to them, 'Then give to Caesar what is Caesar's, and to God what is God's.' (Luke 20:23–25)

Every Sunday, when millions of Christians focus on what Christ has achieved for them, many of them remind themselves of spiritual truth by handling mundane objects – a piece of bread, and a cup of wine.

Although all of these sources can provide material that could be used to illuminate a point, it is important to choose examples that will mean something to the hearers. A church I once attended ran a class for young preachers. It makes me blush now to remember the practice sermon I gave. As a student, I had just spent a term studying the poetry of Gerard Manley Hopkins (a Roman Catholic priest, whose poetry is not renowned for its ease or popular appeal). In the sermon I referred to an incident in one of his poems where the Virgin Mary appears to some distressed people in a shipwreck to give them comfort, and I likened this to Christ standing beside us in our own times of distress. The tutor tactfully pointed out that the people in the small, independent evangelical churches of rural Norfolk that I would be preaching in were unlikely to have read the work of a complex nineteenth-century poet, and that, as keen Protestants, they certainly wouldn't appreciate Christ being compared to the Virgin Mary!

What means something to you won't necessarily mean the same thing to others. The more you know your audience, the more likely you are to be able to match your material to their backgrounds.

Some things to do

1. **Read through Matthew's Gospel and identify the examples used by Jesus. Can you find any other sources of examples that Jesus chose from, other than those categorized above?**

2. **Set up a filing system and start to build up your own library of examples.**

3. **Prepare two versions of an evangelistic talk aimed at completely different audiences – for example, for a youth group and for a service at an old people's home. Adapt the core material by changing the advance organizers and the illustrations.**

CHAPTER 7

CHOICE WORDS

Overview

Have you noticed that the language used in churches is often so different from the language used outside? And I'm not just talking about swearing! For instance, we go to a doctor, but we feel the need to refer to Jesus as the 'Great Physician'. And we may talk about 'being washed in the blood', but this could give quite the wrong impression to many people who may not understand what we are talking about.

Does it really matter, or is it just a trivial issue of taste?

- This chapter begins by looking briefly at some of the mistaken beliefs that people have about religious language.
- It continues by considering in detail how choice of language can influence communication.
- Chapter 8 concludes the argument by looking at how religious language can contribute to positive or negative impressions of God.

Thinking where to put your feet

For most of us words come naturally, don't they? It's usually only in situations of intense emotion or embarrassment (such as when trying to comfort a grieving relative) or in situations of conscious creative endeavour (such as when writing a book) that the flow seems to dry up. There are times when words are almost part of our automatic behaviour, like changing gear in a car. We sometimes find ourselves conscious of having spoken only *after* the event.

Running is also a fairly natural activity that most of us are able to do (for short periods, at least). We run when we have to (such as at 10:29 on a Sunday morning) without too much thought about where to put our feet. But for the Olympic athlete, such attention to detail is crucial if he or she is intending to go for gold. If we take communication seriously we need to become more conscious of our language and more proficient in word-crafting.

When we use language we are both creating and dressing-up our thoughts. There are some occasions where 'formal' dress is expected and other occasions where 'informal' dress may be more appropriate. Someone who says: 'It is extremely necessary for you to refrain from committing sins which derive from the carnal nature of the Old Adam and which pollute the sanctity of the matrimonial bed' is dressing the communication rather formally and pompously. On the other hand, someone who says: 'Stop having sex with your neighbour's wife' is being informal and slightly shocking.

> *We need to develop skill in choosing words carefully. If we choose the wrong words people will feel uneasy and we will almost certainly be misunderstood.*

Language and magic

Some Christians genuinely believe that some kind of special 'religious-speak' has to be used. They argue that we take care to be formal with our language when we are addressing somebody important. How much more should we address God in language which reflects his importance! The language we use to or about God, they say, must be different and 'superior'. Regardless of the degree of formality in the context, religious language should consist of formal vocabulary, elegant and carefully constructed sentences, rhythmic prose, and even particular intonation patterns. In this way the religious content of the language is kept from being profaned by contact with the 'vulgar tongue'.

It is easy to see how this kind of religious language can become distant from the language spoken by the average member of the congregation. And as the language begins to sound less natural and more difficult to understand, the words themselves begin to take on a mystic power of their own – almost a magical power.

Some people come to believe that the words can have an influence, regardless of understanding. Passages of 'Scripture' are quoted or printed and stuck everywhere with little attempt to explain them in twentieth-century language to the spiritually blind. The words themselves ought to be enough. It would be sacrilegious to some to suggest that the words ought to be paraphrased. (Unfortunately the story of Philip and the Ethiopian eunuch is somehow forgotten.) Other people come to believe that they are helped merely by reciting partly understood religious phrases. For others, liturgy can have an aesthetic attraction regardless of faith or understanding.

The objections to making religious language more 'user-friendly' are flawed in two important respects. First, the last half-century of linguistic research has shown that all languages and social or geographical dialects have extensive vocabularies and subtle grammars. There is no such thing as a linguistically 'superior' language or dialect.

But perhaps the most convincing reason is the example of Jesus. He could have taught in liturgical Hebrew, but he chose to speak in Aramaic, the everyday language of the people. The Aramaic term 'Abba' is preserved even in a gospel written for Greek speakers (Mark 14:36). Jesus clearly showed that he was concerned with using direct, memorable language that ordinary people could relate to.

- He could express abstract concepts in concrete terms taken from everyday life.

    'Out of the overflow of the heart the mouth speaks' (Matthew 12:34).

    'You cannot serve both God and Money' (Matthew 6:24).

- He used imagery which was fresh and memorable.

    'You are the salt of the earth' (Matthew 5:13).

    'I am the gate for the sheep' (John 10:7).

- He wasn't afraid of using humour to help reinforce a point.

    'How can you say to your brother, "Let me take the speck out of your eye," when all the time there is a plank in your own eye?' (Matthew 7:4).

    'It is easier for a camel to go through the eye of a needle than for a rich man to enter the kingdom of God' (Matthew 19:24).

- He appeals to simple common sense.

    'How can the guests of the bridegroom mourn while he is with them?' (Matthew 9:15).

    'No-one sews a patch of unshrunk cloth on an old garment' (Matthew 9:16).

- He is capable of being blunt.

    'You of little faith' (Matthew 16:8).

    'You hypocrites!' (Matthew 15:7).

    'Do you still not understand?' (Matthew 16:9).

- Sometimes his language is hauntingly puzzling in order to stimulate thought.

    'Blessed are the meek, for they will inherit the earth' (Matthew 5:5).

    'Who is my mother?' (Matthew 12:48).

God doesn't need the protection or the fancy dress of special language. He wants to be talked about and understood.

Language and understanding

Did you know that a 'mouse' is a palm-sized pointing device for touching the cursor on a computer display screen, as well as being a cheese-nibbling rodent? And did you know that in addition to being a male sheep a 'ram' is a semi-conductor storage device whose cells can be accessed in any order?

If you are familiar with these two terms of computer jargon, you're probably also aware of such wonderful terms as 'expansion bus', 'floppy', 'rom', and 'megabyte'. If, on the other hand, you have so far succeeded in avoiding reading popular computing monthlies and have progressed no further than a joystick and a fairground racetrack simulation, the terms mentioned above would be either meaningless to you, or misunderstood by you.

If you have trouble reading about, or listening to talk about, a subject that you are unfamiliar with, just pause and think for a moment about the trouble that some people have when they listen to a sermon or attempt to read the Bible.

When thinking about religious language and understanding there are at least three main problem areas.

Problem 1: culture

Have you ever tried to read an English translation of a novel that was originally written in Russian, Polish, or Japanese? If you have you'll know that often the difficulty you soon encounter is not so much with the translation, but with the complexity of the place or character names. And then, sooner or later, the more subtle sources of cultural confusion inevitably arise. What does that ritual mean? Why do the characters keep referring to that event in their past history? Why are they tolerant of behaviour that I find so shocking?

Anyone reading or listening to Christian communication is bound to face language about concepts and events from a completely different culture. The stories of the Bible are miles away geographically and at least 1900 years distant historically from modern-day Europe or North America or Australia. The hearts of Old Testament patriarchs, fifth-century BC housewives, first-century AD fishermen, Egyptian Pharaohs, Babylonian and Jewish kings, Ethiopian court officials, and Roman centurions may be very similar to our own hearts in many respects. However, in spite of the internal similarities, the external fabric of *our* lives, and our social assumptions and knowledge, are extremely different. This presents a large cultural barrier that the communicator has to cross.

Christian communication often seems heavily loaded with words and concepts from another time and another place. On an obvious level, some words can seem very strange and uninviting to the uninitiated. For example:

> Bethel, Jehosophat, Jezreel, Asherah, Baal, Purim,
> sabbath, Armageddon, Pharisee, centurion, tithe.

On a more subtle level, an understanding of Jewish religion and culture is clearly going to be necessary if the language relating to practices such as 'circumcision', 'sacrifice', and 'offerings' is to be appreciated. And there are countless examples where a greater appreciation of the social, political, and historical contexts of particular books and passages would help us better interpret the significance of their words (for example, the obligations of men to their widowed sisters-in-law, Matthew 22:24).

Problem 2: specialized subject-matter

All subjects have specialist vocabulary associated with them. Children's misunderstandings of religious subject vocabulary has produced many apocryphal stories in Christian humour. You've doubtless heard about the little boy who started addressing God as 'Harold' ('Our Father, who art in heaven, hallowed/Harold be thy name . . .'). And then there's the one about the little girl who came home from Sunday School crying and protesting that she didn't want to become a vicious old man ('I will make you fishers of men/vicious old men, if you follow me . . .').

And it's not just that children sometimes have problems

65

understanding the religious *words*. The religious *concepts* can be quite baffling, even when the words are relatively simple. One child actually asked: 'If Jesus lives in me, does it mean that when I eat my tea it goes all over him?'

In spite of the jokes there's a serious issue. How many adults could explain what 'hallowed' means? When talking to each other two computer buffs don't need to stop and explain terminology every time they mention a word which is used mainly in computing circles. When writing or talking to those who understand something about God we can assume some degree of understanding of theological and biblical terminology. However, to the outsider, a sermon which is riddled with such terms as 'redemption', 'justification', 'predestination', 'mortification', and 'omnipresence' can appear to be in a foreign language. It may sound full of sound and fury, but it would signify very little.

Problem 3: familiar words

Surprisingly, it's not always the foreign-sounding names or the long theological terms that cause the problems. Sometimes the small or common words can cause just as much misunderstanding. In some ways they are more troublesome because the difficulty is less immediately apparent. I'm thinking of words such as:

heaven, hell, election, save, flesh, wrath, fall, love.

Each one of these words would be readily understood by most people, and yet unconverted people are likely to understand the words differently from most Christians.

Words are like onions: they have several different layers of meaning. It is helpful to be able to think of the difference between *denotative* and *connotative* meaning.

- *Denotative*: Broadly speaking, denotative meaning is the dictionary meaning. It is the meaning of a word which the vast majority of language users would agree on.
- *Connotative*: Connotative meaning is determined, not

by common consent, but by my own past experience. Because of particular associations some words mean things to me that other people don't share.

Because of these layers of meaning, several people could agree on the denotative meaning of a word, but in addition have totally different understandings of the word based on connotative meaning. We might all agree that 'dog' meant something like: 'quadruped of many breeds, having characteristics $x, y, z, etc.$' But if you have spent many happy years in the company of a playful, protective, and faithful friend called Rover, you are likely to have a different understanding of the word 'dog' from somebody who was savagely attacked by such an animal as a child.

When communicating we need to be on the look-out for simple terms which may be grossly misunderstood by those who do not share our background experience. To take an extreme example, a woman who has been sexually abused as a child may have difficulty in immediately warming to the concept of God as a loving father. A more common example can be seen in the way in which non-Christians misunderstand the Christian concept of 'love'. If Christ's apparently simple command to 'love our neighbour' is to be understood, we need to convey to people that 'love' means more than 'nice feelings' or 'sex'.

> *Words are like books – each chapter represents a different meaning. The effective communicator has to remember that some members of the audience don't always own the books that are treasured and dog-eared in the speaker's library. And even when the audience has the same books as the speaker, the communicator has to ensure that everybody has the same book open at the same page.*

Some things to do

1. Look again at the brief analysis of the language of Jesus on page 63. Read through Luke's Gospel and find other

examples to go under the given headings. You may need to invent new categories to cover aspects of the language that you find.

2. Find a friend who loves you enough to be honest with you (Proverbs 27:5–6). Make a recording of a talk or sermon that you have given and get your friend to listen to it with you. Try to answer the following questions:

   a Are the speech rhythms natural, or are they false and chant-like? Do you sound as though you are trying to imitate a Derek Nimmo impersonation of a member of the clergy?

   b. What cultural or theological terms need further explanation?

   c. Are there any words which unbelievers might interpret differently from you?

CHAPTER 8

WORDS ANCIENT, NOT MODERN

The days are gone when irreverent teenagers had good reason to laugh at some of the more outmoded phrases produced by a religious culture that had been dominated by the Authorized Version of the Bible. The people of the 'press' who prevented Jesus from going about his business (Mark 2:4) have rightly been replaced by the 'crowd' of modern translations. Similarly, the clockwork device used by the undertakers in Acts 5:6 ('they wound him up') has been replaced by more suitable references to the wrapping of the body.

The Authorized Version of 1611 was greatly influenced by Tyndale's translation of 1526. Tyndale's aim had been to produce a translation that a ploughboy would understand. In spite of this heritage, and in spite of the ability of biblical writers to communicate powerfully within their own cultures, many of us today may occasionally fall into the trap of dressing our message in faded suits, moth-balled crinolines, and archaic corsets.

One of the most noticeable features of religious language that we may find ourselves using frequently is the once

69

vibrant but now worn-out and tired phrase. In a large number of cases these phrases have been lifted straight from the Authorized Version. Often the original meaning (and certainly the original vitality) has been lost.

Whereas it is at least arguable that the analogy of God as a successful and humanitarian industrialist may have a freshness that is worth exploring, his owning 'the cattle on a thousand hills' has become romanticized and hackneyed. How many speakers, let alone the congregation, understand references to Christ as 'the Rose of Sharon'? And what exactly are 'scarlet sins'? (Is there any connection with 'scarlet women' that grandmother used to mention with such distaste?) The frequent repetition of phrases such as 'Bless you!', 'Praise be!', 'Praise the Lord!' ('PTL'), and 'Hallelujah!' may assist social cohesion, but the almost ritual reciting of religious formulas can lack meaning. Over-use is also helping to devalue some adjectives, such as 'precious' and 'almighty'. In 'precious blood' and 'Almighty God' they are beginning to have little more modifying force than 'nice'.

Some of the worst clichés are those religious-sounding euphemisms where an archaic phrase has been preserved in order to make something relatively mundane appear holy. We may find ourselves encouraging people to 'do visitation' rather than to 'visit'. In a country where viticulture is rare we may insist on seeing ourselves as part of a 'vineyard' which, if the prayers of the 'saints' are anything to go by, has innumerable 'corners'.

And what about the unfortunate people who are ill? If they are described as languishing 'in sickness', their condition seems worse than it is. 'Illness' is gradually replacing 'sickness', leaving the latter word with a more specific meaning. Not only are ill people 'in sickness', they are often 'laid aside in beds' of it!

When reading the Bible, we may encourage the faithful not to 'understand' but to 'profit from' or 'glean from' the 'Scriptures'. After their public reading the hope may be expressed that God would mysteriously 'add his blessing'.

While it may be possible to appreciate the Old Testament

pressure to turn a simple gift into an 'offering', a slight sense of menace rather than of religious worship may be conveyed when the congregation learn that the 'offering' will be 'taken up'. In many churches the process is performed by stewards who will 'wait on you'. They will wait *for* you while you fumble with coins or notes, but they certainly will not serve you dinner.

As well as containing annoying, baffling, or amusing clichés, religious language often conveys a sense of age. Along with aspects of content discussed in the previous chapter, this contributes to the image of Christianity as foreign and old-fashioned and helps to distance the message from the contemporary reader or listener.

In discussing quantity, 'superfluity' is rarely heard these days in church (do you remember being intrigued by 'super-fluity of naughtiness'?), but 'abundance', 'abounding', and 'multitude' are quite common in Christian parlance. The nouns used for human suffering not only reflect the frequency of occurrence of the experience, but also the language of 1611. 'Bondage', 'chastisement', 'longsuffering', 'travail', 'tribulation', and 'affliction' are not words in common use. Other ageing nouns used in some circles include 'partaker', 'hereafter', 'supplication', 'edification', and 'blessedness'. And while today we may be used to having 'enemies', these often become 'adversaries' in church.

Some of the verbs sound equally strange. We may ask new converts to 'give a testimony' rather than (more naturally) to 'testify'. We may describe this process as 'witnessing', and the uninitiated may be forgiven for asking, 'Witnessing what?' It is also virtually impossible to simply 'look for' people. We sometimes feel it necessary to 'seek' them in a poetic way. 'Seek' is often used as well to convey part of the meaning of one of its archaic forms (beseech), as in 'seek for forgiveness'. Outside church we 'stay': inside we 'abide'.

Part of the strangeness of the language arises from the differences of culture and the subject-matter being considered. But in some cases more modern or easier terms could be found for describing the divine. For example, 'longsuffering' and 'lovingkindness' could shed their archaic clothes quite easily without too much loss of meaning. Words such as 'righteousness', 'justification', and 'sanctification' need changing. 'Righteousness' has come to have unhelpful associations with 'self-righteousness' and connotations of priggishness. I have often found that the use of 'justification' and 'sanctification' leads to 'mystification'. All three terms would sound very formal and antiquated to a single mum who left school at sixteen and who reads a tabloid newspaper, and to other more educated and socially advantaged listeners from a non-Christian background. 'Advocate' is used more frequently as a verb than a noun these days, so it would make more sense to describe Christ in his mediatorial role as a 'mediator' or 'barrister'. Faced with a mystery, few of us would naturally turn to 'unsearchable' or the unnecessarily poetic 'wondrous' to describe the phenomenon.

There are at least five reasons why some communicators cling to ageing language. One explanation is the security that is found in staying with tradition. A second reason may be the comparative isolation of some of the speakers. The people with the most power to determine the linguistic culture of a church, the ministers, can sadly be the ones who are most isolated from non-church contacts, and are also the ones most likely to spend time reading religious books. As has been argued, another reason for resisting change may be a genuine but mistaken desire to use unusual language as a way of showing respect for God.

The two final reasons may be those which are common to most high priests of linguistic subcultures everywhere: a subtle pride in the mastery of the language of the initiated, and a forgetfulness about how strange it may seem to the outsider.

In his book *Evangelism in the Early Church*, Michael Green describes the evangelistic zeal of Irenaeus:

> He made a practice of preaching in the villages as well
> as the towns of Gaul where he was bishop, and did so,
> not only in Greek, the language which many of the

educated inhabitants would understand, but also in the vernacular. Such was his concern to fulfil the evangelistic role of bishop that he took the trouble to learn and become fluent in the language of the despised barbarians, of whom even the best pagan philanthropists took no account.[1]

While many of us will not be expected to learn a new language in order to preach the gospel, we may well need to take more account of the linguistic subculture of our audience if we are to communicate effectively with them.

We need to repent if we have encouraged people to take God less than seriously because of our contribution to an impression of him as being dated and quaintly archaic. We should not continue to lumber people with the linguistic baggage of the early seventeenth century. Paul changed the presentation of his message to suit the context because he wanted to be an effective communicator in order to make disciples. We should adjust our language accordingly.

Some things to do

1. Make two columns in your notebook, and listen again (with a friend if possible) to that recording of yourself giving a talk or sermon. Every time you hear a stale cliché, stop the machine and write it down. In the opposite column, write a word or phrase that would have been fresher and more meaningful – if the cliché needs replacing at all!

2. Look carefully at a church magazine or set of printed notices. What words are used which indicate that the typical writers and readers of such documents are members of a subculture which is failing to communicate in modern English?

THE HIDDEN PERSUADERS IN CHURCH

Overview

Why is it that we are sometimes angered, not so much by what the speaker says, as by the way she or he says it? And why do some well constructed messages often fail to have the impact that they should?

The German philosopher, Nietzsche, said of Christians: 'I would believe in their salvation if they looked a little more like people who had been saved.' This chapter and the next look at the power of non-verbal communication. Chapter 9 looks at the hidden messages that a church can give, and chapter 10 goes on to consider the importance of non-verbal communication for individual speakers.

Non-verbal messages and churches

Somewhere near you?

One Sunday morning at eleven o'clock, Sandra, a young mother with two toddlers, staggered into church. Three weeks previously her 'husband' had left her. Having just moved into the area, and knowing no-one to turn to, she had phoned the number on the church notice-board. She was desperate for help. The church was on the main road, just before the turn-off on to Sandra's estate. She had noticed it several times on her bus ride back from town.

During those three weeks Eric and Ruth had made frequent visits. They had shown down-to-earth, practical love, and they had spoken very gently about God's love for her. Sandra was slightly impressed, in spite of herself. Even apart from what they said they had communicated that she was important, and that they cared.

On this particular Sunday morning, without being invited, she had turned up to church out of gratitude, guilt, boredom, and curiosity. Eric and Ruth were not there on this occasion, but they realized that she must have attended from the description some friends gave them of the 'woman with the two kids'. They were thrilled, even though they were surprised that nobody could remember her name.

That joy soon turned sour when they next visited Sandra. For nearly an hour she gave them an angry blow-by-blow account of what had happened and of why she was never going to *that* church again. Although Eric and Ruth realized that Sandra's anger must have made her exaggerate somewhat, they found themselves feeling increasingly ashamed as the story unfolded. That hour of bitterness arose for the following reasons:

1. She was greeted at the door by a stern-faced man who mumbled something about the service already having started. She could see he was alarmed by the children. There were no seats at the back for late-comers and she was herded down to the front just as the service began. She 'nearly died of embarrassment'. Having struggled for the past hour to get the children ready, she felt that she was now being punished for being late.

2. There were no crèche facilities. She had to sit and fight to keep two bored toddlers quiet for an hour and a quarter. The only 'help' she got was a faint smile from the pulpit and a few glares from the rows behind her.

3. There was nothing in the service for the children to listen to or relate to.

4. She noticed that all of the men were wearing suits and that a large proportion of the women were wearing hats. Sandra felt uncomfortable. She hadn't got a hat and she certainly wasn't going to buy one. And suits made her think of Mormons and double glazing.

5. About half-way through, her anger and unease turned to panic as she realized that she hadn't got any collection money. She couldn't face looking at the stern-faced man as she quickly passed the bag back to him.

6. The Bible and hymns seemed so old-fashioned. She couldn't understand much of what was being read, or much of what she was trying to sing.

7. Even she could tell the piano was out of tune.

8. Everybody looked so miserable.

9. The building was cold and dingy. It had been built about 150 years ago. It hadn't been refurbished in that time, and it hadn't been decorated for about twenty years.

10. The preacher was boring. He certainly wasn't excited or moved by what he was saying. His reading from his notes lacked conviction. He didn't look at his audience, and just droned on in a dead pan voice.

11. At the end of the service she was either studiously ignored, or smiled at nervously. Nobody asked her name, and nobody offered her a lift home.

Eric felt that it was inappropriate to ask her if she actually listened to what the preacher said.

Somewhere else near you?

One Sunday morning at eleven o'clock, the same Sandra, a young mother with two toddlers, staggered into church.

Eric and Ruth were away on this occasion, but they visited Sandra at home during the next week. For nearly an hour she gave them an excited blow-by-blow account of what had happened and of why she wanted to come to their church again. Although Eric and Ruth realized that Sandra's excitement must have made her exaggerate somewhat, they found themselves feeling increasingly thrilled and proud of their brothers and sisters as the story unfolded. There were several factors that contributed to that hour of excitement, surprise, and opportunity. Eric and Ruth could see that God had been working, and they also knew that the verbal messages had been reinforced and strengthened by non-verbal ones.

1. She was greeted by a confident and smiling couple. They sympathized with the problems that Sandra must have had in getting the children ready, and reassured her that it didn't matter that the service had just started. The lady explained that the church had a crèche, that Sandra was welcome to stay with the children, but that if she wished to leave them with the supervisor there were seats at the back for parents and late-comers. The lady also discreetly told her where the toilets were. Sandra listened to the service for about ten minutes in the crèche while the toddlers settled. The church had obviously bought a lot of equipment for the children, and the supervisor was so good that Sandra was soon able to leave them and slip into the back of the service.

2. Sandra arrived just in time for the talk for the older children. She couldn't believe it. Her memories of a few times at Sunday School were of wet-looking pictures of Jesus and decorated texts in blue and gold. Here, there was a husband and wife team teaching the children a modern song and telling a very funny story about a boy and girl who lived on a housing estate. As well as being enthralled by the story Sandra was really impressed with their overhead projector transparencies. Somebody had taken a lot of trouble to prepare something really interesting.

3. She noticed how relaxed everybody seemed. Some people were really formally dressed. Others were dressed very casually. There didn't appear to be any 'official uniform'. There was certainly plenty of variety and Sandra didn't feel out of place.

4. She panicked slightly when somebody stood up and drew attention to the notice sheet. She remembered that 'notices' usually meant 'collection', and she had forgotten to bring any money with her. However, when the man soon sat

down, nobody started to collect money. Sandra thought: 'This church really is different!'

5. She was both pleased and frightened by the books she had been given at the door. One of them was a Bible, and she had wanted to try and follow what was being read. But she was concerned she would look a fool by not knowing what page to turn to. She needn't have worried, as the lady reading the lesson announced the page number in the church Bibles before she started. And Sandra was startled when the lady started to read. It sounded so modern. It was as if God was speaking to her in her own language. And the hymns and choruses were also so different from what she expected. The tunes seemed contemporary and the words weren't archaic. They spoke directly about real feelings that Sandra was beginning to want to identify with.

6. One of the things that really excited her was the worship. There was a whole range of musicians and the singing really went well. And people seemed to be involved in what they were doing. There was a sense of joy, enthusiasm, and expectation as people sang to God. You could see from their faces that they were doing something that they really believed in. Sandra wanted to know more.

7. The building was pleasantly warm without being stuffy. The seats were comfortable, and the furniture and decor were modern. There was carpet on the floor. The atmosphere was 'inviting'. Sandra felt relaxed and welcomed.

8. And the preacher was so good! By the time the sermon came round Sandra wanted to listen. She felt intrigued. She was already impressed and predisposed to listen. He didn't drone on for hours. His points were clear and relevant. It wasn't unstructured religious waffle, academic irrelevance, or insultingly simple anecdotes. Sandra felt helped by what he said. She could sense that he had something real and important to say. The congregation actually laughed at some of the jokes and responded intently to his sincerity. He looked at people. His voice wasn't flat. A few days later she would be able to tell Eric and Ruth what he had said. A few

weeks later she would still remember that he spoke with authority and conviction.

9. Within minutes of the service finishing several people spoke to her and took an interest without intruding. She was invited back for coffee. She was given a lift home.

After listening for nearly an hour Ruth felt that it was appropriate to invite her to church again, and to begin to probe a bit more deeply about her response to what the preacher had said.

The hidden messages

Your church may not be like either of the two extremes described above, but every church gives off hidden messages that either help or hinder the Christian message. What are the hidden messages in your church?

- Does it communicate to parents that children are important and welcome, or does it discourage parents from coming to church?
- Does it go out of its way to make visitors unwelcome through its choice of people at the door, or through not having a humane seating policy?
- Does it communicate the message that God is continually hard up for money, and that people have to give?
- Does it implicitly give the message that people must wear a 'uniform' before they are accepted?
- Does it make people feel physically uncomfortable through neglect of heating, inappropriate seating, and dismal decor? Would you be embarrassed if your living room was heated, furnished, and decorated to the same standards as your church?
- If a stranger were to watch people coming from your church, would he feel that the people had been to a meeting with an important and inspiring leader who was alive and real? Is there as much excitement, enthusiasm, involvement, and commitment as there is at an average political rally?

- Does your church give out the message that good music is unimportant?
- Does your church let strangers know that they are welcome and important?
- To the many professional people who might consider coming, does it give the impression that it couldn't organize a Sunday School party for five children well, and that lack of planning and sloppy administration are the norm?

CHAPTER *10*

MORE SOURCES OF NON-VERBAL MESSAGES

The power beyond words

One of the ways we communicate with people is by speech. We spend hours preparing the messages we want to give, but we tend to lose sight of the importance of the non-verbal parts of our message. We concentrate on making our meaning clear and hope that our words will convey the meaning we want. But speech is only part of our meaning-explaining activity.

In many situations, speech is the *least* important part in the communication process. The power of non-verbal communication is greater than the power of verbal communication. Michael Argyle, Professor of Psychology at Oxford University, has suggested that in some circumstances, non-verbal messages are sixteen times as strong as verbal ones.[1]

Although this may seem shocking at first, it becomes more plausible with a little reflection. Think about some of the speakers you have listened to over the last few years. I suspect that you will be able to remember an impression of many of them without remembering much of the specific content of their messages. Of my own memories, two in particular stand out. One is of a very arrogant and sarcastic preacher who annoyed me intensely, and the other is of a very godly and humble man whose presence I found humbling and challenging. I can't remember anything of what either of them said, but they communicated powerfully through non-verbal signals such as smiles or frowns, volume and tone. If you think back to the last church business meeting or Parochial Church Council meeting you went to, you may find it difficult to remember what was said, but you will certainly remember whether you felt the speakers were friendly, hostile, or indifferent.

In effective communication the verbal and non-verbal messages support each other. In ineffective communication, not only does that mutual support break down, but non-verbal communication can work to positively undermine what is being spoken or written. And given the power of non-verbal communication, it can completely destroy the usefulness of our carefully prepared message.

I could say to somebody: 'Welcome back, it's good to see you again,' and I could support this message in the following ways:

- By causing my face to radiate a warm and open smile and by meeting his or her eyes with mine.
- By moving nearer to the person I am talking to.
- By giving a hug or a handshake (depending on the age, sex, and sensitivity of the person and my knowledge of him or her).

Alternatively, I could say: 'Welcome back, it's good to see you again,' and destroy the meaning of the words in the following ways:

- By having a smile that never reaches my eyes, which remain cold and hostile, and by ensuring that my eyes never meet those of the person I'm talking to.
- By moving away, or by leaning back with a stiff and tense body.
- By refusing to offer a handshake.

The listener is convinced by the smile, or lack of it, not by the meaning of the words.

Think about the way we sometimes present musical items in

church. How often do we lack conviction or authority and fail to communicate effectively? If we do, it is rarely because of the words we sing or because of the quality of the music. It's almost certainly caused by the looks of nervousness, embarrassment, or indifference shown on our faces and by the way we stand.

If we are to get better at communicating Christian truth it is essential that we develop our abilities to recognize and use hidden messages. What I want to do in the remainder of this chapter is to outline the major sources of non-verbal messages.

Key sources of non-verbal messages

Speech

Apart from the actual meaning of the words themselves, we convey many messages in our speech. When two teachers say to similar classes of rowdy children, 'Be quiet and sit down!', two different results may be achieved. The children recognize when the important note of authority and confidence is in the delivery of the words and when it is absent.

Tone: Some of the most important messages carried in speech delivery are provided by tone. Think about how the following could be spoken in completely different ways, even though the words are the same:

They were unfriendly.

They were unfriendly?

They were unfriendly!

Unfortunately, speakers often fail to use tone to its full advantage. When reading the Bible in public, some speakers fail to think about the changes in delivery needed to convey questions, commands, or quiet authoritative statements. At a more serious level, failure to attend to tone can 'kill' the whole message. When preaching against sin, a serious and sympathetic tone would help the message: a sarcastic one would destroy it. If you are depressed, don't speak in a depressed way; you'll just depress your audience. If you are full of joy, be careful that your elation doesn't ride roughshod over bleeding hearts.

Volume: Another important feature of speech delivery is volume. We can use differences in volume to emphasize certain points and to demonstrate emotion. As a general rule, the anger of the speaker is usually associated with increases in volume, and tenderness with quietness. The Bible talks about shouting for joy and there are times when we may naturally reflect our excitement and emotion in the loudness of our speech. A sudden increase in volume may awake the sleepers and emphasize a point, but an equally effective way of emphasizing the point (if not of waking the sleepers) is to suddenly drop the volume. There can be great power in softly spoken words provided that there is sufficient volume for all to hear.

Don't forget two very basic points. First, always speak loudly enough for all people to hear. If you haven't got any elderly people sitting on the back row, imagine them, assuming that at least one is slightly deaf, and speak to them. People will become annoyed if they can't hear you.

Second, don't make the mistake of assuming that loudness means you will automatically be heard. Too much noise can be counter-productive. People do not like being shouted at, especially in confined spaces!

I well remember going to an open-air meeting. The leader handed the microphone to a young preacher who proceeded to *shout* into it. The volume was such that everybody within a 300-mile radius could hear the noise, but few, if any, were listening. Most people walked by very quickly. On another occasion a different preacher spoke very naturally into the microphone. He wasn't trying to reach China from England, and there were certainly people in the distance who couldn't hear him speaking. But people started to come closer to find out what he was saying. He was using natural curiosity to attract.

Diction: My wife Nina often tells me that she can't hear me at home. My problem isn't so much volume, as poor diction. Poor diction means mumbling in such a way that the consonant sounds become indistinct. In a public meeting, if you mumble, they will grumble! I usually remember to enunciate clearly at church but become inarticulate at home.

Consonants are crucial in helping us to identify what people are saying. When you listen to people with a different accent you can usually understand what they are saying even though their vowel sounds may be quite different from yours.

In conversation it is quite normal to miss some consonant sounds out or to change them in some way. We often don't pronounce the final 'd' sound in 'and', for example. But if we are in a hurry and excited, or if we are shy and lacking confidence in what we are saying, we may unconsciously start to 'swallow' too many sounds. There is a performance aspect to public speaking. We don't need to make ourselves sound silly, but we do need to take care to open our mouths and move our lips more than usual.

Tempo: Variations in speed of delivery provide another subtle source of meaning in speech. It is possible to speed up or slow down the rate at which syllables, words, and whole sentences are produced. Different speeds can convey different messages. A sentence spoken with extra speed can convey urgency; one spoken at a slower speed can convey emphasis or deliberation. A rapid, clipped style can convey irritation. Drawls can be tedious to listen to. Again, variety is the key.

Accent: There is a widely held belief that there is such a thing as 'correct' English (including 'correct' pronunciation). People who deviate from it are often caricatured as slightly mentally deficient or of shady morals. For years linguists have been arguing that there are many regional and social varieties of English. All such varieties are governed by rules and make sense. It is pointless to talk about 'superiority' and 'inferiority'. All that this does is reveal our own social prejudices. It is much better to talk about 'appropriate' and 'inappropriate' language. Unfortunately, it is a fact of life that many people will quickly make some very superficial assessment about us on the basis of our accent.

The whole matter of accent and communication effectiveness is further complicated by the issue of social class. There are certain language features which members of one class are more likely to adopt than members of another class. In Britain and America, for example, the pronunciation of the 'ng' sound in words such as 'coming' and 'going' is one such feature. Some people regularly pronounce the 'ng', while others would regularly say 'comin'' and 'goin''.

Whenever we open our mouths people will make intuitive judgments about our regional and social background. This can work to our advantage. If we come from a rural community and have a strong regional accent, we may more easily gain acceptance when speaking to people from that community. On the other hand, if we speak to the same group of people in Received Pronunciation we may unintentionally cause hackles to rise.

We are what we are – part of God's varied creation. Our accents reflect that diversity. We should be aware of the accent we have and be sensitive to those times when we may have to try harder to establish our credibility because of it. But we shouldn't become over-sensitive about it. We should also avoid putting on a carefully modulated 'telephone voice' in church and try to remain natural. (Some would argue that there is a definite phenomenon known as 'Anglican-talk'.) We should never pretend to be something that we are not.

Touch

Sending messages by touch is limited by strong taboos or conventions about body contact. These limitations are necessary because touch can carry such powerful meanings of aggression or warmth. Our society allows us to express warmth to strangers of both sexes through handshakes. As speakers we should use this channel to strengthen bonds with our listeners. I suspect that our reception would be improved if we could find a way of shaking hands with people as they came into the meeting, rather than when they left. We should also resist the meaningless handshake. Reinforce the message of the hands with the words of the mouth and the interest in the eyes.

Gaze

I well remember one speaker who always avoided looking at the congregation by staring out of one of the side windows as he spoke. As a result of this many people spent the entire sermon looking at the same side window wondering what was going on outside that was so transfixing the speaker.

By looking at people we tell them that they are important. The very act of looking implies interest and recognition.

During conversation most of us recognize the importance of gaze and can use it quite naturally. When we are being spoken to we tend to look at the person who is speaking. That person in turn will give us occasional glances, but will not look directly at us for long periods. However, when that person is ready to hand the conversation back to us and indicate that it is now our turn to speak, he or she will look directly at us for a longer period. As listeners we usually gaze for long periods: as speakers we usually glance fleetingly.

In conversation we break these norms only under very special circumstances. As listeners we may wish to convey indifference or hostility to what is being said and we will look away from the speaker. (Congregations start looking at their watches or staring at the floor.) As speakers we may wish to convey affection or a certain amount of aggression and will look intently at the people we are talking to for longer periods. Lovers and teachers know how to look people in the eyes to reinforce appropriate verbal messages. If we look away when listening, or stare when speaking, people normally start to feel uneasy. Sometimes people may appear to be either cold or rude. Part of the problem may be inappropriate gaze patterns. If we have developed inappropriate gaze patterns it really is worth working to change them.

Gaze is also crucial to the communication process when we are talking to groups of people. We can use it to encourage discussion in small groups. We should make a point of looking encouragingly at the person who is offering us a contribution in response to one of our discussion questions. To look away, or to look with disdain, would encourage the contributor to stop. With children we can use the eyes to control. Looking at a child for anything longer than six seconds is a powerful way of indicating disapproval.

When giving a talk or preaching we *must* look at the people we are talking to. We shouldn't stare at them but should look fleetingly at a wide range of people (not just the ones at the back). We should try to use our eyes to draw people in to what we are saying. The emphasis we want to come across is 'I am giving this message *to you*', rather than 'I am giving this message'.

Wherever possible in house meetings, arrange the seating so that you can see everybody.

Gestures

Every society develops gestures which carry a specific meaning for that group of people. In Britain there are about twenty such gestures that could be used, but the people of Naples have approximately 200 to choose from.

When we speak to an audience we tend to use gestures that do not have meanings in themselves. Instead they take their meaning from their relationship to our speech. They amplify and elaborate the spoken word. Some people use them to indicate heightened emotion; others use them to emphasize certain words or phrases; others use them to emphasize certain divisions in a structure or list. Part of Billy Graham's skill as a speaker is his ability to punctuate and reinforce his points through hand gestures.

You've doubtless heard the story about the preacher who wrote on the side of his sermon notes: 'Argument weak here. Shout loudly and thump the pulpit.' I'm not for a moment suggesting that we should rehearse gestures before a mirror, or that we should use them to try to hide a weak argument. On the other hand, we should not be afraid to use them. We should preach with the whole body and if we feel strongly about something, we shouldn't feel restrained about using our hands (or legs) to reinforce what we are saying.

Proximity

Generally speaking, the more we like a person and the more we are interested in what she or he may be saying, the closer we move to that person. On the other hand, if we do not wish to convey intimacy, interest, or friendship we keep our distance. Although pulpits will strive to lift you up and keep you away from people, try to get close to them when speaking, if possible. When speaking to small congregations I will always ask if they mind if I don't use the pulpit. They will invariably agree and allow me to speak from a place much closer to them. (And if the congregation won't move to the front, I always move to the back!)

Orientation

The way in which we position ourselves in relation to others and handle the space around us gives off various messages. Asking someone to sit next to you gives a different relationship with him or her from sitting opposite the person with a desk between you. You can stand in front of a group behind a desk or pulpit, or you can sit in a circle surrounded by the same group of people. The differences in orientation will produce vast differences in the type of meeting and the learning processes that follow.

If we want people to relax and feel that they can contribute something to the meeting it is best to sit in a circle. If we want people to listen and not talk, it is best to sit them in rows directly opposite the speaker who should be standing. Ministers sometimes despair over people who will contribute to discussion and pray out loud on a Wednesday night at a house meeting, but who refuse to do the same on Sundays. Part of the answer is to do with the difference in the formality of the two meetings. The numbers of people at the meetings play a part, but orientation is also a crucial factor.

I once preached in a church that had acute orientation confusion which contributed to severe communication weakening! The church had started as a house group and, when forced to meet in a larger building because of numbers, the members naturally wanted to retain as much as possible of the informal house atmosphere. They met in a thin, long room, which unfortunately didn't lend itself to circular arrangement. So a compromise had to be reached, and the chairs were arranged in the way indicated below.

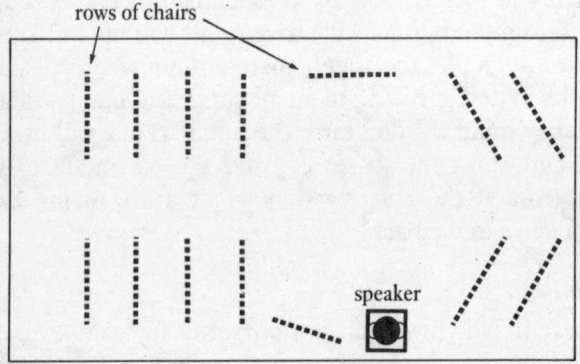

The result was that they had produced a situation in which it was very difficult to preach and look at the congregation.

One of the best evangelistic meetings I ever went to was in a community centre on a large council housing estate. The building was crowded with people who had come to a 'Family Rendezvous' as part of a church mission. After an hour of family games, followed by a filmstrip, the evangelist got up to speak. It could have been disastrous. The non-Christians were on home ground and had had an hour of fairly lively fun. People drew their chairs around the front table when asked to and within seconds the speaker had them almost eating out of his hands. With a broad smile he stood up, moved round the front of the table, perched himself casually on the corner and said: 'I want to tell you about the time I spent a night in gaol for something I hadn't done . . .' Now admittedly he did have a good story to tell and he was able to identify with his audience, but the warmth of his smile, his physical closeness to the people, and his casual approach all helped him to win a hearing.

Physical appearance

As with accent, people will make superficial judgments about us on the basis of our appearance. We are able to control our appearance much more easily than our accents, even though we cannot change our basic physique. We make decisions as to the kind of image we present to people through our clothes, our hair, and to some extent through the use or non-use of cosmetics. The clothes we wear to a particular occasion give clues about how we see the situation and how we intend to relate to the people there. The most obvious message coming from appearance relates to the degree of formality we wish to present. As a member of a congregation I try to be tidy and informal in my dress. As a speaker I would dress more formally for a church service because I wouldn't want people to be offended by my casualness. As a speaker at a youth club I would revert to being tidy but informal because I wouldn't want to alienate through formality. Men are often able to regulate the degree of formality at the meeting itself much more easily than women. A man can easily take off a jacket or loosen a tie.

All of us can smile quite easily, and smiles communicate warmth, regardless of the formality. There is a world of difference between being serious and frowning. Frowning usually indicates hostility or anger.

> *For too long we have been preoccupied with the content of verbal messages and have neglected the power of non-verbal ones. We need to produce newsletters that enhance the message they contain and do not hinder it. We need buildings that communicate warmth and a level of organization that demonstrates care through the small details. And in such buildings and organizations we need people whose whole being proclaims Christ. Words are only one part of our message.*

Some things to do

1. Think of people you enjoy listening to and try to identify what it is in their non-verbal communication that makes them good speakers.

2. Get an honest friend to tell you about your own non-verbal communication. What are the problem areas that you need to work on?

3. Collect as many examples of non-verbal communication as you can from the Bible. Here are a few to get you started: Matthew 6:17–18; Luke 22:61; John 13:1–18; 1 Corinthians 16:20; Galatians 2:9; 1 Thessalonians 5:22; 1 Timothy 2:9.

11

LANGUAGE FOR LEARNING: QUESTIONS AND GROUPS

Overview

Have you heard the classic definition of a lecture? – 'The transmission of information from the notes of the speaker into the files of the audience without passing through the minds of either speaker or hearers.'

Most communicators know that physically hearing or reading a message doesn't mean that people would necessarily take it in, even if they could understand it. We know all about being on 'automatic pilot' as listeners, even if we tell ourselves that our minds are always fully engaged as speakers. We have already looked at ways of encouraging the reader or listener to understand and remember the message through the use of structure, illustrations, organizers, and appropriate verbal and non-verbal behaviour. What I want to do in the next two chapters is to examine three final ways of helping people to receive the messages we wish to convey.

- In this chapter I try to show the importance of getting the listeners to play an active *spoken* part in the learning process. People who sit in silence are

not helping themselves to learn.
- ■ In the next chapter I suggest ways in which we can help people remember material.
- ■ I also argue for the need to use more than one channel for communicating a message.

Language for learning

What would be the more effective way of teaching you something: to have you listen to a talk about the topic, or to have you listen to a talk and then discuss the topic with somebody else?

If you go into any good school classroom, or read any material on effective educational practice, you may be surprised at the amount of pupil talking that is encouraged. This is because educationalists are now aware of a function for language in education which had previously been ignored by many teachers in the last century and for the first half of this one.

Language is important in conveying information, and in creating a favourable image. But in education, language has more functions than simply carrying intellectual baggage or wrapping up ideas. Language is a tool for learning, as well as content to be learned. By answering questions on what we have learned, and by being encouraged to put into language what we understand and to discuss its implications, we are actually strengthening the learning process. It is now being recognized that some of the most effective education takes place when the learners actually have to use language *themselves* to express what they are learning and to solve problems rather than when they simply listen to the language of others. In other words, the old idea that good teaching consists of addressing learners who always sit in silence and passively listen simply isn't true (though the learners will need to sit in silence for some of the time).

In talking about a topic learners will be answering such questions as: What does this mean? How does it relate to what I already know? What are the implications for me?

Which parts don't I understand? As learners try to formulate their language in discussion with others, they are crystallizing and reinforcing what they have learned, as well as highlighting any misunderstanding or gaps that need further teaching.

Such an opportunity is rarely given in church. Churches tend to value the language of the speaker and undervalue the language of the learners.

The differences between the two approaches to learning can be summarized in the following ways:

Transmission teaching[1]

Typical situation: a lecture.

The language of the teacher is highly prized as containing all the truth and the language of the receivers is discouraged and ignored. Emphasis is placed on imparting accurate information in a logical manner. Listeners are expected to receive this information without question. It is assumed that they will understand it and it will be considered their own inadequacy if they don't. Listeners are to be passive and silent.

Interpretation teaching[1]

Typical situation: a well led group discussion.

The language of the teacher is highly prized, but the experience and understanding of the listeners is also regarded as important. Emphasis is placed on individuals relating the truth to their own experience and, because of this, discussion may be more anecdotal than analytical. Listeners are expected to check understanding and to assess and apply truth. Areas of misunderstanding or poor communication on the part of the speaker will be highlighted. Listeners are to be active and vocal.

Maintaining the status quo

Why would most speakers prefer to give a talk on a topic rather than set up a learning situation in which the audience are expected to talk or write as well as listen? There must be several reasons. I have thought of three.

First, many people would argue that because the practice isn't in the Bible, it shouldn't be attempted. Leaving aside the counter-argument that there are several other church practices that are not in the Bible, it is possible to make out a strong case for the inclusion of opportunities for learner language use in the teaching process. It is clear that as the disciples walked along dusty roads between sermons and later sat together to eat, they talked about what Jesus was teaching and what some of the implications were for their lives. After at least one sermon they realized that they didn't understand and sought further clarification (Mark 4:10–20), and on another occasion their discussion revealed that they had got hold of the wrong end of the stick and needed further teaching (Mark 8:14–21). In addition to his sermons, Jesus clearly often questioned the group to encourage them to put into words what they understood (Mark 8:27–30). The disciples were not just passive listeners in the way in which large numbers of churchgoers are. The New Testament certainly supports the view that many people have contributions to make. It is difficult to read letters such as 1 Corinthians and Colossians and maintain the view that all teaching was done by one man doing all the talking all of the time.

Secondly, many would argue that the Bible acknowledges that some people have the gift of teaching and that these people should be allowed to get on with it. Teachers are to teach and listeners are to listen. The idea of ordinary members of the congregation (horror of horrors – even women!) chipping in with their two-pennyworth seems totally unbiblical.

I agree whole-heartedly that encouraging people to use language in an unguided way can be a complete waste of time. But I am not arguing for this. I am suggesting that people should be helped to reflect on the meaning of what they have listened to or read through sensitive and structured questioning as prompts for discussion or writing. The questions could be written down, or they could come from an appointed leader. The person giving the initial teaching would almost certainly be the person to guide the questioning. The questions are to be seen as a continuation of the teaching process and not as something in opposition to it. Teachers are still teaching: they are just varying their methods.

Thirdly, churches are very conservative places and some are unlikely to seriously contemplate the idea of changing the learning format on occasions.

Creating language opportunities

We need to create ordered situations in which learners are encouraged to ask questions and shape their understanding in words. In most cases opportunity for this can be most easily constructed in a mid-week meeting rather than in a public service on a Sunday. (Though if the organizers of large Christian conventions can create such opportunities with thousands of people, most churches could manage it on a Sunday if they thought it was appropriate.)

Here are some suggestions for helping listeners bring their own language to the learning process.

1. If you speak regularly at one particular church, try to encourage people to make notes during the sermon. It doesn't matter that they are likely to lose the notes or never consult them. The act of writing in their own words what you are saying helps to reinforce understanding. You could use the back of the notice sheet to give questions for people to consider as they listen.

2. On occasions, provide listeners with worksheets containing questions to fill in at home. This provides a framework for encouraging learners to continue to reflect on what has been said and for applying it to their own lives. If you are conducting a series of mid-week meetings you can emphasize the importance of individual reflection at home by making sure that group members have opportunity to discuss with a partner, or in small groups, what they have written (if appropriate) at the beginning of the next meeting.

3. Provide time and create opportunities for structured discussion at the end of your talk. This is more easily done in

home groups. I have found three things particularly helpful. First, it is best to keep groups small (ideally four and no bigger than six people). Secondly, give printed questions with space for written answers. This helps to focus attention on the task in hand. Thirdly, always try to have a plenary session where one person from each small group reports back to the larger group at the end of the session. This encourages the leader of the small group to move the discussion along and stick to the questions because the leader knows that she or he is going to have to give a public account of what the group has discussed. It also gives you information about what has been understood or misunderstood, and about which groups are working well together.

4. If it is not possible to provide opportunities for talking or writing, you can certainly encourage learners to think about what you are saying by asking rhetorical questions. Jesus often used questions to encourage his listeners to reach conclusions for themselves and to be involved in the learning process (for example Matthew 6:26–28; 16:26).

> *You and I learn more when we are encouraged to become involved in the learning process, and when we are asked to use language in relation to a topic we inevitably become involved in that process. As communicators we need to focus on how to give learners an opportunity to use language, as well as on what we have to say.*

The art of questioning

If we want to encourage people to use language as a tool for learning we will also need to pay careful attention to the kind of questions we give as a basis for discussion or writing. Bad questions will either bore or confuse, and, as I hope to show in the Appendix, it is possible to answer some questions correctly without necessarily having any understanding of the topic concerned.

Some questions do little to help learning because they are

so ambiguous. They leave people wondering what precisely is meant and this leaves them feeling frustrated. For example, it was obvious *to you* that when you spoke on John 9 and asked your small groups to summarize the reactions of the people to Jesus, you were referring to the reactions of the Pharisees. But you shouldn't have been surprised that the groups spent twenty minutes discussing whether or not you meant the reactions of the Pharisees, of the disciples, of the man's parents, of his neighbours, or of the crowd.

Other questions fail because they are almost an insult to the intelligence of the learners. The answers are so obvious that they are hardly worth giving, and in a group situation, people will not want to state the obvious and will start to get resentful or bored.

We can divide questions up into two or three types. Some educationalists talk about 'open' and 'closed' questions. Closed questions are ones which have a right or wrong answer. The answers are usually of a factual nature and can be fairly obvious to anyone who has read the passage or listened to the talk. They are 'closed' questions because the response the learners can give is restricted. They either know the answer or they don't. There is little room for any interesting discussion or negotiation about possible meaning. Examples of closed questions would be:

- In John 9:41, what did Jesus say to the Jews?
- What qualities does love have, according to 1 Corinthians 13:4–7?

Closed questions can be very useful in helping learners to establish a factual framework of essential details (what happens, and who says what to whom). They give apprehensive people something easy to think about. However, they don't encourage learners to think beyond the obvious in order to get to grips with the deeper meaning, or to apply the lessons at a personal level. Closed questions don't generate much language for learning.

Although they are more difficult to answer, open questions tend to stimulate much more thought and discussion. They are 'open' because there is no single answer which is right or wrong. With closed questions learners find a particular answer from something written in front of them or from what they have just heard: in open questions learners have to search their own experience and reading to come up with possibilities. They have to draw evidence together and make inferences about character and meaning; they have to explain and evaluate. Examples of open questions would be:

- What do you think Jesus meant when he said: 'I tell you the truth, if anyone keeps my word, he will never see death' (John 8:51)?
- Read Daniel 1 (in particular Daniel 1:8). In what areas of your own life do you need to make a stand for what you believe in? What does Daniel have to teach us about how to stand on principle?

Using a slightly different analysis of the learning situation, comprehension theorists argue that in order to help people understand we need to ask literal questions, inferential questions, and evaluative questions. We need to move beyond the tasks that simply require the regurgitation of facts and encourage learners to 'read between the lines'. Learners should be encouraged to infer meaning, to draw conclusions, to evaluate the effectiveness of an argument. In a Christian context we could add practical questions. We want to make sure that our learners understand the consequences of the teaching for their own lives.

Table 1 is an attempt to summarize the different ways of analysing questions that have been discussed above.

Language and groups

It is also worth mentioning briefly two other factors which will encourage learners to use language. The first concerns the way in which leaders respond to the language that learners have produced either in writing or in discussion. In order to encourage discussion, group leaders need to follow a few simple rules. Even the best questions will produce only silence if the following guidelines are ignored.

1. Pay very close attention to the non-verbal elements of

Table 1: Different types of question

	Question type	**Example**
CLOSED	Literal	*What did Jesus say?*
CLOSED	Simple inferential	*Why do you think Jesus wept at the tomb of Lazarus?*
OPEN	Complex inferential	*What did Jesus mean by his statement here?* *What kind of man was Daniel?*
OPEN	Evaluative	*How successful was Moses as a leader?*
OPEN	Practical	*How does your prayer life need to change in the light of Daniel 9?*

the discussion. Make sure that people are comfortable and are sitting where they can see each other. You need to create a climate where potential contributors feel relaxed and valued. You won't encourage discussion by sitting down with a frown. People won't want to speak if they see you fiddling with papers, yawning, or looking out of the window while they are talking. Attend to what they are saying and give encouraging nods and smiles.

2. On occasions throughout the discussion thank people for their contributions. Even if you disagree with what some people are saying you can genuinely thank them for making a contribution. They won't necessarily have found it easy to share their thoughts before a group.

- *'Thanks, Sue, for saying that. I'm sure that the difficulty you have put your finger on is shared by many. I've certainly had problems with that point.'*
- *'Thanks, Karen. That helpfully brings together lots of the reasons given in the passage.'*
- *'Thanks, John. I know that some people may not agree*

with you about that, but I appreciate your honesty in sharing your views.'

■ *'Thanks, Richard, for saying that. I take your point about the millennium being related to our main topic of personal evangelism. I'd like to stick with evangelism in this passage at the moment, but we can come back to your point at the end, or perhaps consider it as a separate topic next week. I think if we tried to tackle it now we might miss the force of what this passage is saying.'*

3. One certain way to make people feel defensive and cautious is to judge or evaluate what they are saying too quickly. It is extremely important to indicate that we wish to understand what someone is saying *before* we pass comment on it. We can check with the speaker that we have understood their contribution by paraphrasing their message. We can discuss with the speaker and check that we have understood their real message and feelings.

Consider the following situation. Imagine that you have spent some time discussing Mark 5 with a group. You ask them to consider the implications of Mark 5:19 where Jesus tells the delivered demoniac, Legion, to go home to his family and tell them how much the Lord has done for him. You ask a good open, practical question: 'What kinds of things could *we* do in order to put verse 19 into practice?' At this point Richard jumps in with, 'I can't tell my parents about my faith!' How do you respond?

You could judge his response too quickly and give a reply which indicates that you think he is wrong. 'It may be difficult, but we have to share our faith with our family. That's what part of being a Christian is.' Richard feels despised and angry, and thinks that you have not heard what he was really saying. He won't try to make helpful contributions again for this session and he may not come to the group again.

You could show you value his contribution and then try to get at his real meaning. 'Richard has been honest enough to share his difficulties over this verse. I wonder, Richard, if you could explain a bit more about what you mean. Do you mean "I can't because I don't think it would work", or "I can't because I'm afraid to", or "I can't because I don't know how"? Or do you mean something else?' In this way you show you value Richard's spoken contribution and genuinely want to understand what he is saying. It turned out that Richard meant he didn't know how to share his faith with his family. You were able to get some practical suggestions from the rest of the group and in the process, you succeeded in getting an answer to the original question. If Richard had meant something different you could have used the experiences of the group to help deal with Richard's problem before returning to the main question.

4. If, after making sure that you have understood what somebody is really saying, you feel that you have to make a negative evaluation of their comments because what they have said is clearly contrary to the Bible or is unhelpful, try to do it graciously. Again, wherever possible, I try to draw the rest of the group into the discussion. 'Karen has said that she thinks these verses mean XYZ. How do the rest of you feel about that? Does it correspond to what you think? Can you think of any verses that would support or challenge this interpretation?' In this way I am acknowledging Karen's contribution and at the same time am hoping to show her that several of us think she is mistaken here, and that the reason we think so is because of what the Bible teaches. She is more likely to willingly accept the judgment of her peers and the authority of the Bible than to accept my telling her she is wrong!

Exactly the same principles apply on the few occasions when we may see what people have written in response to questions we set on a previous occasion. We need to communicate to people that we accept and value their contributions, even if we don't always agree with them. We should always allow people the non-threatening options of either not writing at all if they don't want to, or of not having to read out what they may have written.

A few pages ago I hinted that there was another factor likely to encourage people to use language in order to learn. I was thinking of their own experience of having done just that. The more we work in groups, the better we get at it. Good group discussion doesn't happen overnight. It has to be worked at. The questions need to be appropriate. The leader needs to be skilful. And the members need to have grown to know and trust each other. They also need commitment to what they are doing and this is most likely to come from successful learning experiences in groups. We talk most to people we respect and trust in a relaxed atmosphere. But relationships, trust and commitment take time to build, so don't be discouraged during the first six months.

Getting people to use their own language to help learning can be difficult. We need to be aware of the potential effects of different types of question and ask ones which are likely to provoke thought and encourage response. What people say or write needs handling with care and sensitivity, and group members need time to develop group experience.

Some things to do

1. Take the topic of 'discipleship', and research some material to teach an average congregation for twenty minutes. Produce both a sermon outline, and a sheet containing questions for group discussion. Remember to include both open and closed questions.

2. Study the questions in some commercially produced group Bible study material. Analyse the questions according to the categories given on page 101. What questions would you want to change?

3. If you get a chance to lead a group Bible study, ask your best friend to evaluate how you handled the responses that people made.

4. Plan how to communicate a message in church avoiding the traditional 'unsupported talking head' method, *i.e.* just one person talking without using any other media.

5. **Further reading.** There are several excellent books that will give you further practical help with some of the suggestions given in this chapter. Two that I have found most useful are:

   - *Lead Out: a guide for leading discussion groups* (NavPress, 1974).
   - *Use Your Overhead: over 100 ideas* by Lee Green (Victor Books, 1979, distributed by Scripture Press).

CHAPTER *12*

HOW MEMORABLE ARE YOU?

We have considered several ways of making your material meaningful, and hence memorable.

- In chapters 4 and 5 we looked at the importance of structure in helping us interpret information. If the material rambles aimlessly we will have to work hard to impose some sort of order on it to get any meaning from it.

- In chapter 6 we considered how to relate the material to what the listener already knows.

- In chapters 7 and 8 we looked at the need to use language which is clear and which doesn't alienate.

- In chapters 9 and 10 we considered the importance of reinforcing verbal meaning with appropriate non-verbal behaviour.

- As we have seen in chapter 11, being asked to talk or write about something also helps us understand meaning, and this in turn strengthens our memory of the material. For instance, you are more likely to remember the content of this book if you follow the suggestions given in the 'Some things to do' sections than if you don't.

Do you repeat yourself?

Another way of helping people to learn material is to use *repetition* as a means of reinforcing memory. In broad terms, whether or not we remember something hinges on two things: the material has to be something we can understand, and we need repeated exposure to it.

It isn't enough for the material to be meaningful. We need to see or hear it for longer than a few seconds if we are to remember it for any length of time. And the longer and the more complex the material, the greater the exposure to it we need if we are to retain it. A speaker who packs three points into a twenty-minute talk is more likely to have her material remembered than a speaker who tries to pack nine points into the same time. This is partly because few of us are likely to be able to repeat a list of nine points unless we had spent some considerable time learning the list (as for an exam) whereas most of us could remember three quite easily. Another crucial difference is that someone who spends twenty minutes discussing only three points is likely to give more explanation and repetition of each of those points than someone who is trying to cover nine in the same time.

Jesus seems to have been fully aware of the importance of memory. Not only did he tell stories that drew on people's everyday experiences, not only did he give clear teaching that addressed itself to people's deepest needs, not only did he make pithy, memorable statements, he also repeated himself in order to drive home a point. We find him repeating the same text on more than one occasion (Matthew 9:13; 12:7). Some would argue that the sermon given by Jesus in Luke 6:20–49 is a repeat of a sermon given on a different occasion in Matthew 5, 6 and 7, with at least part of the congregation being identical on both occasions. We can be certain that the feeding of the 4,000 in Mark 8:1–10 is a separate event from the feeding of the 5,000 in Mark 6:30–44. It is clear from the comments in Mark 8:14–21 that Jesus was expecting the disciples to learn something from the two demonstrations of his power. As well as meeting human needs, he repeated the miracle in order to help the disciples grasp a point and remember a lesson.

The strongest evidence for Jesus' use of repetition comes from some of the parables where we sometimes see him repeating similar points in a variety of ways. In Luke 15 we have the parable of the lost sheep, the lost coin, and the lost son. Although it could be argued that the parable of the lost son emphasizes different points from the other two, there is sufficient common ground in the parables to see that Jesus was hammering at least part of his message home in three ways.

I know that arguments from silence are weak. But it doesn't seem unreasonable to suggest that more repeated teaching may have been discarded and lost with the 'many other things' (John 21:25) when the gospel writers came to edit their material.

I have listed below some practical ways of repeating material.

1. Follow the example of Jesus and don't be afraid of using two or more stories to illustrate the same teaching at different points in the service or message. For example, in family services I prefer to avoid a long sermon, and divide my material up into three chunks which are interspersed throughout the service. Having decided on a key message that I want to get across, I then invent or borrow two stories that illustrate my main point. I make sure that one story is aimed at the four- to seven-year-olds, and that one is aimed at the eights to twelves. These two stories become two of my speaking chunks. The third one is the same material applied to teens and adults. This means that the congregation gets the same core message in three ways during the service.

2. Try to build into your talks places where you pause and *briefly* recap what you have said before going on to the new material. You need to be able to stop and summarize. This is important in writing, but it is even more important in speaking because the words are quickly lost and cannot be returned to unless the speaker resurrects them. The best places to do this are at the end of major sections in your talk.

*We've spent some time thinking about what Christian for-
giveness doesn't mean. Among other things, we've seen that it
doesn't mean forgiving reluctantly or grudgingly and that it
doesn't mean imposing limitations on what can be forgiven. In
the time that remains I want us to consider two positive points
about Christian forgiveness.*

This practice is valuable for communication because it
both reminds the audience of the structure of the message
(and thus aids comprehension of the material) and repeats
key points (thus helping the audience remember them). In
this book I have deliberately tried to summarize key points
throughout the text and have occasionally tried to summarize
longer sections of argument (see the opening page of this
chapter, for example). My close friends have told me that the
practice can be extremely tedious and counter-productive
when speaking if it is done too often. Pause to summarize at
the end of *major sections* of a talk and *not* at the end of every
point.

3. One of the most effective ways of repeating material is
to use a variety of media for presenting that material. This
will be the subject of the final section of this chapter.

A multi-media approach

In church, most of us choose to channel our message through
one medium. We simply speak. If we have a message from
God to deliver, we stand and say what our message is and
hope that a few might appreciate our effort and remember
our words. For most of the time we ignore alternative
channels of communication. The trouble is that by failing to
exploit all the channels that are available to communicators
living at the end of the twentieth century, we also fail to
communicate as effectively as we might.

I recently attended a conference where three people led a
two-hour seminar. At the end of the session, instead of
feeling bored, I left feeling exhilarated, challenged, educated,
and stimulated to find out more. During the session, each

speaker had spoken for no more than twenty minutes. One speaker had outlined general principles; another had taken these principles and applied them to one particular area of work; the third had also taken the principles and applied them to a different area. The formal presentations were punctuated by small-group work where we were expected to discuss and jot down answers to carefully prepared questions designed to encourage us to apply the material to our own situations. The talks were also punctuated by several opportunities for the whole group to ask the speakers questions. As we entered the room we were given booklets containing the outline of the talks as well as relevant maps, diagrams, and pictures to help us follow the speakers. One of the speakers used colourful and professionally produced sheets on the overhead projector which enabled him to simplify a considerable amount of complex material. Another speaker used a tape-slide sequence to illustrate his argument. The third speaker adopted a completely different approach. Instead of adopting a discursive approach she conveyed her material by graphically describing several real-life situations as examples of the points she wished to convey.

The whole session commanded my respect, and the non-verbal communication 'shouted' that here was a group of people who really wanted to teach me something important and who had spent a lot of time planning this learning experience for me. But in addition to being impressed, I had actually learned something that was relevant to me, and had been stimulated to follow up the session by rereading the notes and searching for other material. The organizers had used a variety of media and a range of learning experiences to repeat the message and to prevent my interest from dropping. Instead of just being asked to listen to an argument, I was offered stories as well. I also saw pictures and diagrams. I heard music. I was encouraged to speak and write things down. I had material to read.

I have seen it argued[1] that we remember approximately

10% of what we *read*

20% of what we *hear*,

30% of what we *see*, and

50% of what we *see and hear*.

Although I am sceptical about the precision of these figures, my experience as a teacher and learner would suggest that the proportions are probably correct. We certainly remember more of what we see and hear than of what we just hear. Unfortunately, Christian communicators are generally reluctant to use more than spoken language to communicate a message.

Of course, Jesus never used an overhead projector, but in an age that lacked acetate sheets and cheap paper he certainly used pictures. His teaching is full of visual material. As has been argued in chapter 6, Jesus painted pictures with words. Not only that, he actually handled or was able to point to children, coins, fish, bread, sheep, doors, wells, flowers, and camels which served as visual aids. Occasionally he also acted out things he wanted to teach, as when he washed the disciples' feet (John 13:1–17).

The practical details of how to use other media could fill another book, but here are just a few ideas.

1. Use an overhead projector to reveal progressively the structure of your talk, to display appropriate quotations, charts, diagrams, maps, pictures.

2. Photocopy appropriate sheets to give to your audience. Be aware that if you give out sheets *before* the talk, your listeners may switch off. On most occasions it is best to use the overhead projector to reveal material during a talk and photocopied sheets to follow up content after it has been delivered.

3. Why not think more often about cutting down the amount you say and of giving some of the time to an appropriate filmstrip or video? If based on the content of the visual material, your reduced words are likely to be very effective.

4. If your church has creative talent that can be controlled and channelled, set up groups to help you. In addition to a music group, you could have an art/printing group to serve the church through the production of visuals, and a drama group to deliver occasional sketches with a message that you could build on in your talk.

5. Use lots of visuals and participation when talking to children. When speaking to very young children try using puppets.[2]

13

BEING AND BECOMING: AUTHORITATIVE COMMUNICATION

Introduction

With some communicators you not only listen, you also want to do what they say or you feel incredibly guilty about not doing it. Why do some speakers seem to have so much more authority than others?

Words, pictures, smiles, and types of argument are all tangible. We can isolate and dissect them at leisure. I have tried to show that by identifying particular factors and by consciously controlling them, we can make communication much more effective.

There are some elements in communication, however, that are not so easy to control consciously. They have more to do with our character than our performance skills on a particular occasion. They are to do with factors that can change slowly over time, but which are unlikely to change dramatically overnight. What I want to do in this chapter is to attempt to analyse what it is that contributes to authoritative communication.

The importance of authority

On many occasions the effectiveness of a talk is determined, *not* by the content or delivery, but by whether or not the audience sees the speaker as having authority. No matter how polished your performance, if people don't respect you, they won't listen. They might hang around and tolerate your words entering their ears, but most words would be quickly dismissed before there was any chance of them ever getting near the heart or will. If you are an unknown speaker, you might be able to establish your authority once you have started to speak. However, in many cases where you are known, the battle will have been largely lost or won before you stand up.

Again, enter God

Ultimately, any spiritual authority we have as communicators comes from God. He can work through natural means to give us authority in our messages. On the other hand he can ignore natural means and choose to give us 'something special' in spite of ourselves, usually for a particular purpose. But exceptional happenings shouldn't discourage us from trying to improve the norm.

It was one of those evenings when you went to church out of duty rather than out of any sense of expectation. The speaker was a dear brother who had many gifts, but public speaking wasn't one of them. And, of course, nobody in the leadership had had the courage to tell him. But on that night something tremendous happened. We all knew that God had spoken through him. After he started to speak everything seemed to come together. He spoke clearly and with boldness and authority. He looked at people and seemed freed from his notes. There was even real emotion in his voice, usually a flat monotone. God decided to give the church 'something special' on that occasion. For the first time in his years of preaching, people were able to thank him for what he had said without awkwardness. And he was on the mountain top for days afterwards.

About two months later he spoke again. People went to the church with a sense of expectation. But nothing unusual happened, and never did again. He had lost the authority that was clearly supernaturally given to him two months earlier.

God can and does give supernatural authority on occasions. I covet such occasions. However, for a lot of the time he chooses to use less dramatic means for establishing a communicator's authority. I want to consider three areas where we can develop long-term character-building projects to help improve our own authority and therefore our effectiveness.

Authority source 1: credibility

We may be able to think of occasions when we were able to witness effectively to complete strangers whom we 'just happened' to meet only once. But some of the most effective evangelism often takes place when we have earned the right to speak to people. If we take time to get to know people and show that we love them and care about them, they are less likely to refuse an invitation to an evangelistic meal and are more likely to be open to our conversation afterwards, than if we had just put an invitation through their letter-box and run. Our credibility as people gives us authority.

I can remember once when a very gifted evangelist weakened the impact of his message with an off-the-cuff remark that he made at the end of a talk. I had invited a friend, who was a dedicated and conscientious schoolteacher, to hear him. He listened well to the speaker. But then the evangelist started to talk about how he used to teach and how he regarded it as a nine 'til four job so that he could have more time to preach the gospel. I know what he meant, but he gave the impression that he didn't take his professional responsibilities seriously and that he was using his employers to pay his mortgage while his real work took place outside school. My friend left unimpressed. For one person, at least, this evangelist had lost his credibility and left his words without authority.

The same is true of 'non-evangelistic' communication. If people can't respect us, how can we expect them to take what we say seriously? We need to impress people with our general competence, industry, and reliability. I know that my testimony as a Christian would suffer at work if I was continually late, took no initiative, offered no help, produced shoddy work, proved myself to be unreliable, and was unsociable. Similarly at church, I know that if I am the kind of person that takes no initiative in service or sacrifice and attends meetings just to get instead of going to give, if I'm late, if I don't try to excel in doing the jobs that I am given, if I prove myself to be unreliable, or if I become distant or unsociable so that I can't make small-talk as well as preach, my sermons suffer. It isn't because I've got nothing to say or haven't crafted the material, but because my congregation will have begun to lose respect for me as a person and as a Christian.

It is difficult to take seriously an exhortation to pray more from someone who rarely goes to a prayer meeting. Many years ago I knew two speakers from different churches who didn't seem to have the kind of effective ministry that they could have had. They were very different. One was young and educated, the other was retired and had received very little formal education. What they had in common was the fact that their communication was mainly weakened, not so much by their material or even their skill as speakers, but by the fact that they weren't too popular as people. One was a bit of a recluse, difficult to disagree with, and had a reputation for treating his family badly; the other was extremely bitter and was continually moaning about his church and its activities. The sermons of their lives got in the way of their words from the pulpit.

Sometimes we are painfully aware of a lack of credibility. It is usually when we don't practise what we preach, or because we have little experience of what we want to talk about. There are inevitably some topics that are difficult to avoid if we preach regularly to the same congregation and try to teach systematically. It may be possible to ask appropriate people to add to what you are saying by testifying to what they have learned from *their* experience. When I know that my lack of experience makes me vulnerable to possible misinterpretation, I always try to draw on what little experience I have and make particular efforts to avoid appearing glib or trite. If we lack credibility because we don't practise what we preach, the remedy is to start practising.

Although listeners are told not to despise youth, the young preacher, Timothy, is also told to 'watch his life ... closely', because if he does he will save both himself and his hearers (1 Timothy 4:16). We are to be concerned about our reputation. Without a good reputation our communication will lack compelling force.

Authority source 2: knowledge

They say that a little knowledge is a dangerous thing. In communication terms it can be disastrous as well. Would you go to a dentist who wasn't qualified, who was basically a mechanic who had just happened to feel led to be a dentist, who had convinced a few undiscerning people that he ought to be allowed to have a try, and who had opened an eighteenth-century dentistry manual at random in order to discover what to do? You wouldn't trust the person or respect anything he or she had to say about dentistry. And if you wouldn't tolerate such a dentist touching your mouth, why do churches tolerate preachers with little or no training, and with only superficial knowledge, attempting to teach people spiritual truth?

A mistake which often leads to some speakers making themselves look foolish is when they are so transfixed by the text that they ignore its context. Mistakes can easily be made if you fail to apply some basic rules for interpreting the Bible, namely that you can interpret a particular verse correctly only by placing it in context and by comparing it with other Bible passages on the same subject. If you are so preoccupied with preaching on the words of a particular verse you are likely to fail to search widely for other biblical angles on a particular topic. And this material will be found only by systematic study. It is not likely to arrive by waiting to 'feel led' to preach on something, or by reading through a passage in your quiet time in desperation, thinking, 'How can I get a sermon out of this?'

At best, such preaching gives only a partial picture which somebody else *may* be able to complete. At worst, it can give a totally misleading picture that may leave individuals or congregations caught in an unbiblical trap for years.

I don't wish to appear contentious, but several examples spring to mind. Some people get very excited about the gender of God and argue that he chose to reveal himself as a man, and they would wield several texts to support this (*e.g.* Psalm 103:13). However, such a position can only be held if you ignore the fact that he can also be compared to a woman (Luke 15:8), a mother (Isaiah 49:13–15; 66:13), a woman giving birth (Isaiah 42:14), a midwife (Psalm 22:9), and a seamstress (Genesis 3:21). Those who would wish to argue on the basis of 1 Corinthians 14:34 and 1 Timothy 2:11–12 that women should remain silent in church must take into account 1 Corinthians 11:5, where the issue is covering, not speaking, and 1 Corinthians 14:29 which implies that women are to assist in verbally assessing the prophets. They must also take into account all the references to women prophets (*e.g.* Exodus 15:20; Judges 4:4; 2 Kings 22:14; Nehemiah 6:14; Isaiah 8:3; Joel 2:28–29; Acts 21:9).

Anyone who is serious about communicating God's truth needs to be serious about study. Surely part of Christ's authority stemmed from the fact that he knew the Old Testament far better than those around him who were basing false teaching on it. If students are prepared to study in order to gain qualifications for this life, how much more should Christian communicators be prepared to study in order to help people prepare for eternity?

I have three main sources of reading material:

- ■ God's library of sixty-six books (the Bible);
- ■ Basic reference texts such as a concordance, a Bible dictionary, and as many commentaries as possible;
- ■ Books on particular topics.

All Christian communicators need to spend time alone with God on a regular basis to worship him and feed from him. We often communicate best those things which mean something to us. We need to spend time with God's Word, not in order to look for sermons, but just to listen to him. Out of these times understanding will grow, sometimes dramatically, but more usually, gradually. The servant in Isaiah 50:4 regularly listened to God and because of this was able to teach others: 'The Sovereign LORD has given me an instructed tongue, to know the word that sustains the weary. He wakens me morning by morning ... to listen like one being taught.' It's impossible to be dogmatic, but some would claim that anyone who is serious about having any sort of ministry to others ought to be spending *at least* half an hour a day alone with God. I would argue that quality is just as important as quantity. If we wish to have authority as God's messengers we need to be *at least* as serious about studying his Word as the average literature student is about learning his or her set texts (and most would spend longer than half an hour a day with their books).

Many of us who preach or teach in church will not have had a formal theological training, but Paul tells Timothy to watch his life *and doctrine* closely (1 Timothy 4:16). We shouldn't hesitate to consult the wide range of theological expertise readily available to us through reference books[1] or through Bible college correspondence courses.[2] Many speakers would be more convincing if they simply invested the cost of approximately three tanks of petrol in buying a good concordance, a Bible dictionary, and a general Bible commentary. These help me set a particular book or passage in context and give relevant background information. They are also useful in suggesting other passages that are relevant to the one being studied, and in pointing out some of the more obvious pitfalls in interpretation. Good commentaries on the particular books being studied are also invaluable in providing more detailed illumination. They are my basic tools for helping me gather and sift material. They don't always make interesting or devotional reading, and they certainly don't make great sermons. But, they help ensure that the basis for what I have to say is thoroughly biblical. They enable me to dig over the ground and get rid of some weeds and rubbish before planting the seeds. There is no substitute for serious spadework.

My third source of knowledge is books on particular themes or topics (such as 'discipleship', 'personal relationships', 'giving', 'prayer', or 'fasting'). I don't buy these books to 'gut' for sermons, but I find them extremely useful because the author has invariably studied a topic in depth and has used this study, together with his or her own experience, to assemble ideas and passages around a particular subject. At a later date I may want to preach on that topic. When that happens I can use the books in my library as a *starting point* for study. I can look at the headings the author has used and adapt them in the light of my own situation. I can use the index of biblical references to follow up material. They are usually an excellent source of quality material that has been summarized for me. What is particularly useful is to read widely on a particular topic, and to make a point of reading books that you may disagree with. It helps you to see the other side of the argument and makes you evaluate an opposing viewpoint in depth. It may be that you learn something new and end up changing your mind.

Some speakers tend to despise books and boast that all they need is the Word of God. I would argue that reading what others have written about the Word of God, and evaluating it as best one can, is no different from listening to sermons. If I am continually feeding others I continually need to be fed. By reading books I can draw on the knowledge and wisdom of others. When such resources are available it seems tragic not to use them. If the content of our sermons is to command respect, we should want to give people the best that we can. That will involve serious study, and for many communicators, it probably ought to involve buying and reading *at least* one Christian book a month.

Some people read regularly but waste most of their reading because they fail to keep the material they have studied. It is impossible to retain vast quantities of material in our memory without the external support of writing things down. The very act of writing things down also helps us to understand what we are reading. As I mentioned in chapter 6, we need to establish some form of system for recording and filing what we have read. I always read a book with a pencil and piece of paper in hand which I use to jot down the page numbers of passages or ideas that I wish to return to. After completing the book, I use a simple card index box to record the main ideas, illustrations, and Bible references under topics. This enables me to dig out ideas and passages, as well as illustrations, from reading that I have done years previously. If reference books help ensure that my talks have a sound foundation, my filing system helps to provide a good source of bricks with which to build. All these things help my material to have authority.

In addition to attempting to increase our knowledge of God and his Word, we will also command more authority as we grow in our understanding of people. My communication at twenty-eight was a lot more effective than it was when I was eighteen. Part of the reason for that was that I understood more about myself and other people. At eighteen I was just concerned with declaring whatever message I felt God had given me and gave no thought to crafting it, or to how people might respond to it. At twenty-eight I was more aware that people would find certain things that I said to be harsh, or unrealistic, or trite, or just plain ignorant of the reality of their own experience. I had learned to think through what my material would mean to my listeners and to tailor it to what I understood to be their real needs. I remember one speaker reducing a friend to tears because he just hammered home a message that the answer to all our problems was to have more faith. He may be right, but his handling of the material showed a crass insensitivity to the reality of problems that many people face. A more sympathetic awareness of the genuine problems that people have in trying circumstances would have enabled him to offer more concrete and less simplistic suggestions, and would have commanded more respect. We should never lose sight that we are talking to fallen human beings like ourselves.

Authority source 3: the fruit of the Spirit

Some people are very good speakers and yet their ministry often has little impact. It may be that, in God's sovereignty, there will be little visible response. There are countless stories of many godly missionaries and pastors who laboured faithfully for years to apparently little effect. Jeremiah was told that the people would reject his message. For at least one group of speakers, lack of response cannot be associated with lack of spiritual authority.

Before we hide behind that fact, however, let's be honest enough to admit that there are some very good speakers who fail to have a major impact because they lack spiritual substance in their lives. They may have some credibility as people in certain circles, and they may have a knowledge of the Bible, but they fail to change people significantly. I'm thinking particularly of speakers who appear to have a dead orthodoxy. They have been converted. They have grown a little in their Christian lives. They have absorbed their surrounding church culture enough to be able to toe the party line uncritically. They have managed to stop most obvious sinning so that their lives outwardly conform. And for the past ten or twenty or thirty years, that has been that. Spiritual growth has been seen in terms of outward conformity, ignoring the inward heart, and the result has been a growing Pharisaism which is very good at telling people to read the Bible, pray, and stop sinning, but which is very bad at helping people with real hurts. If congregations follow their teaching, it won't be because they are drawn to them as people, or find what they say compellingly attractive.

I'm reminded of the words of a church leader who was responsible for selecting candidates for full-time ministry. He was asked if he would be looking for preaching ability as a main indicator of suitability. The church leader replied: 'The ability to preach isn't too high on my list. You can teach anyone to preach. What I'm looking for is people with broken hearts.' In other words, he was saying that the techniques for effective communication (part of the substance of this book) could be taught and learned by most people, but speakers who were likely to have effective ministries needed to be humble people whom God was working on in depth – people who were significantly showing evidence, not of speaking ability, but of the fruit of the Spirit.

Congregations can be encouraged to change through fear or bullying, but the most effective change is likely to come because people feel drawn to you and what you have to say. I may find you interesting and entertaining to listen to and I may be able to remember what you have to say for months afterwards, but I'm only likely to follow Christ more closely if you have a spiritual authority that has impressed me and convinced me that you genuinely love both Christ and me.

Love shows itself by its actions. One of the best ways that we can increase the effectiveness of what we have to say is by giving ourselves to the congregation that we minister to. I think that there are at least four levels of love-giving and that it is only when we get down to levels three and four that our authority begins to get anywhere near compelling.

Level 1: Giving by what you say publicly

By this I mean regularly attending church meetings with a willingness to participate fully and a desire to make contributions to build others up. If we regularly fail to give to group discussions and to help by participating in times of open prayer, people may find us unconvincing if we suddenly stand up and start to preach. We may feel put out that the church we attend hasn't invited us to lead services and preach. But there may be people who are waiting to point out that however 'gifted' we are, because we are not using opportunities to work to build others up, we would have little authority in the eyes of others to do what we wanted to do.

Level 2: Giving by what you do for the church

By this I mean doing the routine and often unglamorous tasks that are often asked of us as we serve the church. Somebody has to teach the children, bank the money, invite the speakers, unlock the building, lead the Bible study, and clean the toilets. People will respect our labours, particularly if we do them without complaining in a spirit of service and perform them to a high standard for God's glory. People will not listen to our preaching if they think we are proud, lazy, or poor workers.

Many communicators achieve levels 1 and 2 but fail to go further.

Level 3: Giving by what you say and do for individuals

The most effective speakers are those who are sacrificially involved in the individual lives of their hearers, sharing the burdens and joys of singleness and marriage, children and childlessness, work and unemployment, age and youth. Authoritative public ministry grows from strong roots of extensive personal ministry.

So often preachers use preaching and the need for prayer and study as an excuse for removing themselves from their own family and they can become distant from the church. They can appear to be cold and aloof and justify this by telling themselves that their gifts are in preaching and not in pastoral work. While it is true that some may be more gifted in pastoral work than others, there is a sense in which all Christian communicators have to be involved in pastoral work at some level. Although there are times when I long to be able to study and pray more, there comes a point to stop. After a reasonable amount of studying and praying has been done, I have to remind myself that a more effective ministry is likely to come, not through more isolation, but through a visit to a pensioner or through planning a visit to the seaside with my own family and a new family that have just joined the church. Don't use any speaking gift that you may have as an excuse for divorcing yourself from people.

Level 4: Giving by loving attitudes

Paganini, the nineteenth-century violinist, once ended up

giving part of a concert with a one-stringed violin. Although he started the piece with all four strings on his instrument, three of them broke during his performance. To the amazement of the audience, conductor, and the rest of the orchestra, as each string broke, he adapted his fingering and just kept on playing. Charles Swindoll, in his booklet on *Attitudes*, has written that life is 10% what happens to us and 90% how we respond to what happens to us.

Few of us can work in any church for a number of years without apparent justification for disappointment and bitterness. Even if we manage to handle the trials of hurts and frustrations that will inevitably come to us in the course of living, the pains that can be inflicted by churches are often harder to bear. Christians may let us down or betray us. They may say unkind things about us and misinterpret our motives. There is a sense in which some degree of conflict is inevitable. Most human beings find change difficult and preachers are in the business of constantly bringing a life-changing message before people. Not all messages are popular.

Such difficulties can be used to build or to destroy our authority. Remember that you cannot be held responsible for what people say to or about you, but you can be held responsible for your attitude to them. If you use that conflict as an excuse for unnecessary harshness, or constantly snipe back in an attempt to revenge your own pain, you will destroy rather than build up, and your authority will suffer accordingly. If, on the other hand, you are determined to go on loving and building up, God will honour your obedience (John 14:21). Remember, Paul says that love is kind and patient; *it isn't easily angered and it keeps no record of wrongs* (1 Corinthians 13:4–5). Any preacher can love a lovable congregation, and any congregation can love a lovable preacher. But the Christian challenge is for unlovely preachers and unlovely congregations to love each other. It isn't always easy to give to congregations by seeking to build up with loving attitudes, but any authority you hope to keep will depend on it.

We may spend hours crafting messages. However,
to have any life-changing impact, our words need
to be backed by authority. On most occasions this
will depend on God using
  what we know,
  what we do,
  who we are, and
  who we are becoming,
as well as
  what we say and
  how we say it.

Some things to do

1. Consider the differences in likely authority between preaching to your home congregation and preaching in a strange church. What are the advantages and disadvantages in both situations? How could you try to compensate for the disadvantages?

2. Ask an honest and wise friend to help you assess your credibility at church.

3. Ask God to give you more love for your church. Make a list of practical things you could do to show love at levels 3 and 4.

4. How would you seek to improve your authority if you were regularly asked to speak to a group of people whose age or sex (or both) were different from your own? Imagine, for example, that you were an older person being asked to speak to a youth group, or a young man being asked to speak to a group of elderly ladies.

READING FOR LEARNING: PRACTICAL READING ACTIVITIES

Overview

In order to get our message across, we often expect people to read something. Not everybody, however, finds it easy to understand what they read. When working with children, we need to be particularly sensitive to difficulties they may have.

This appendix briefly looks at the readability of different Bible translations. It then goes on to consider a variety of practical ways for helping people get more from their reading. The activities have been designed for use with children. But all of them could be adapted for use with adults, particularly as part of group Bible studies.

Introduction

At the end of my first week of teaching I was summoned into my head teacher's office because of a complaint from an upset parent. My crime? I had asked a fifteen-year-old boy to read a chapter of a novel by Neville Shute for homework.

The parent was not complaining about the fact of homework or about the content of the novel. Her anger was at the fact that her son had been asked to do something which he just could not do, in spite of ten years of formal schooling – namely, read a chapter from a fairly light novel with any degree of confidence or understanding. At first I didn't believe her. Sadly, I soon came to sympathize with her rage. Since then I have been very careful not to make too many assumptions about what children understand from their reading of the Bible.

I once attended a group Bible study at which the leader referred to some verses at the end of Hebrews 10 and asked for a volunteer to read them. While the rest of us sat staring at our shoes a thirteen-year-old-girl tried to be helpful. She strained her way through several verses from the Authorized Version while we admired her courage. She was rightly rewarded with praise when she finished. But the slow and agonizing pace meant that we lost the flow of the writer's argument, and it was clear from her expression that she didn't understand what she was reading either. Her reading may have served a social purpose, but it hindered communication.

Sometimes children have less obvious problems with reading. They seem to be able to pronounce the words with confidence and their fluency betrays few, if any, signs of faltering understanding. But even here there may be a need to be cautious about assuming that they comprehend most of what they are reading. They may simply be doing what some educationalists have described as 'barking at print'. Unfortunately, the correct noise doesn't always correlate with understanding. An examination pass in French may have enabled you to pronounce the items on the menu, but it doesn't necessarily mean that you have too much idea about what you have ordered.

Real reading involves the reader engaging in an intellectual dialogue with the writer. It involves going beyond the form of print to grapple with the substance of what is being said. Children don't always have the intellectual capacity to easily benefit from the sometimes formal and strange language of adult books, or the necessary maturity to understand many of the concepts and apply them to their lives. For many children reading is not an easy activity, and reading the Bible can be an uphill struggle.

Which translation?

Before we look at specific ways to help children learn more from reading the Bible, it is worth briefly considering the use of the Authorized Version. Some people have very strong feelings about the matter and they usually insist that only the AV should be used for public reading and teaching. There are still churches that make a willingness to use the AV a criterion for inviting people to speak.

A few people take a line which comes close to saying: 'The AV was good enough for Paul and therefore it's good enough for me.' Sometimes the resistance to change is shackled with a false emotive argument which tries to sanctify a particular translation: 'It is soaked in the blood of the martyrs!' For those who have reasonably coherent objections the crux of the issue usually centres on the reliability of the manuscripts behind the translations. However, in the light of manuscript discoveries and scholarship since 1611, it seems slightly absurd to maintain that the AV has the best text and that all other translations are corrupt.

My point here is a simple, practical one. Why hinder communication by expecting children to read one of the most difficult translations available? Why deny children access to the Bible's content in language patterns that they are familiar with?

The readability of language can be assessed in several ways. Figures 1 and 2 give the results from two separate attempts to predict the readability level of different translations. Figure 1 shows the predictions for the passages based on factors such as sentence length and word frequency. Figure 2 shows the scores that children achieved on passages from John's Gospel which had every fifth word deleted. The children had to demonstrate their understanding of the passages by supplying

Figure 1
Reading ages for different Bible translations, using the Spache readability formula on samples from John and Ephesians. (This formula is likely to underestimate the real level of difficulty.)

	AV	RSV	NEB	LB	GNB	NIV
John	10.7	10.2	10.9	10.6	9.9	10.5
Ephesians	14.6	13.2	12.0	11.5	11.3	11.9
Average	12.7	11.7	11.5	11.1	10.6	11.2

the missing words. Given the difficulty of the Authorized Version, especially in comparison with the Good News Bible, it seems absurd to use the former with struggling readers.

Reading in worship

I personally feel that children should not (in general) be asked to read lessons in public services. I think that the content is so important that it should only be read by people who are able to communicate its spiritual message. You may disagree with me.

Fortunately there are several things that we can do to help children and adults become more involved in the Bible reading and in understanding what is being read.

Advance organizers

I argued in chapters 4 and 5 that our minds need help if they are to process the streams of incoming language effectively. They need to have 'boxes' ready to receive the information. Anything which gives advance warning of the 'boxes' we are going to need, and which tells us how the new material relates to what we already know, reduces stress and helps understanding. Public reading of the Bible can often be made much more effective from a communication point of view, simply by

having the reader preface the reading with a prepared introduction.

Figure 2
A group of 55 twelve-year-olds' scores from a cloze readability test set on a passage from John.

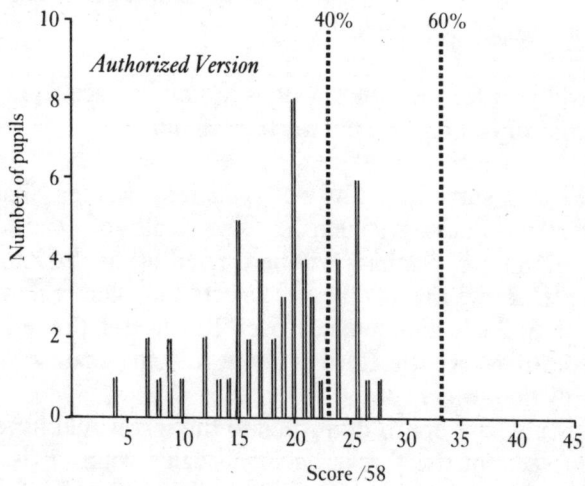

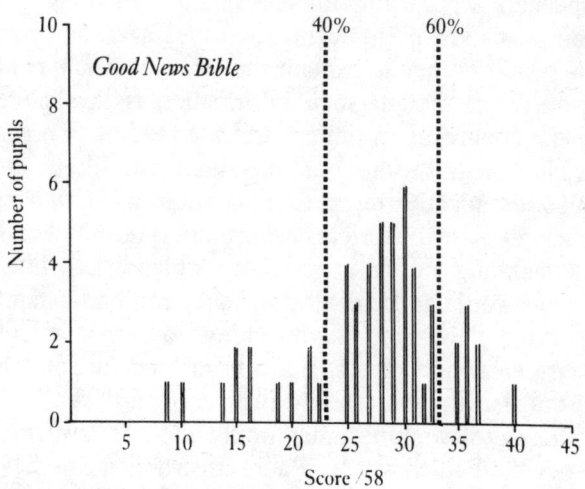

Some passages need the historical context explaining. Listeners need to be made aware of the key characters that are to be named or alluded to in the reading. They also need to know what historical events were important to the writer at the time. An example of where this is fairly obvious is in Isaiah 8. In the middle of that chapter there is one of those verses which tends to leap out of the page and throw itself at preachers desperate for a text:

> I will wait for the LORD, who is hiding his face from the house of Jacob. I will put my trust in him.

However, it is surrounded by words such as 'Maher-Shalal-Hash-Baz', and passages such as: 'The wealth of Damascus and the plunder of Samaria will be carried off by the king of Assyria'; 'Because this people has rejected the gently flowing waters of Shiloah and rejoices over Rezin and the son of Remaliah, therefore the Lord is about to bring against them the mighty floodwaters of the River . . .'.

Clearly any attempt to do justice to the text would have to take into account the threats facing Isaiah's country (Isaiah 8:1–10) and his own personal ministry (Isaiah 8:11ff.). Most good speakers would attempt to explain something of the background at some point during their messages. My point is that few would bother to explain the situation *before* reading the lesson, even though such information is invaluable in helping the congregation understand the reading. To read a chapter like Isaiah 8 without an introduction would be disastrous in communication terms for both adults and children.

In other cases the historical background is not so necessary for understanding, but an introduction which briefly filled in a few details would add greater poignancy and understanding to the passage. Paul's commands on how to behave in Colossians 3 are clear and direct. But a brief introduction which pointed out that the church had just received back the converted runaway slave, Onesimus, would add a certain amount of urgency to Paul's words. Paul's instructions to have a degree of brokenness and humility in relationships, to be willing to forgive 'as Christ has forgiven you', and a surprisingly long section on how slaves are to work, makes even more sense in the light of the tense social situation he was addressing. The Colossian church met in Philemon's home.

Sometimes introductions to readings could be in the form of simple questions that focus the mind on key issues in what is about to be read.

> *Will you turn with me in your Bibles to Paul's first letter to the Thessalonians. (Pause . . .) If you have one of the church Bibles you will find 1 Thessalonians on page 196 in the New Testament. I want to read chapter 2 which is on page 197. (Pause . . .) Paul was writing this letter to a very young church. The people had just become Christians and were facing opposition. The opponents would be telling the new Christians that Paul had tricked them, and that he was just another religious con-man who was only interested in them for what he could get out of them. As I read through chapter 2, try to work out what arguments Paul would use to convince them that he was genuine.*

There is clear evidence in the psychological literature that advance organizers increase the readability of different passages. I suspect that the benefit is even greater for adults or children who may listen to the reading without having a Bible open in front of them. Reading passages from the Bible in public without giving a carefully prepared introduction is to deliver second best in communication terms.

Reading with gaps and gaffes

A very good method for helping listeners focus their attention on the content of a passage, and for helping them to become involved in the reading, is to use a modified form of gap-filling.

This method is not usually suitable for ordinary services, but it can be used very effectively in children's talks and family services. Simply do the following:

1. Tell the children that you are going to read a story and that you want them to listen to it very carefully.

2. Read the story with expression to bring out the meaning, using different voices to emphasize different characters.

3. Tell the children that you are going to read the story again (because it's so important), but that this time they will have to listen very carefully because various mistakes have crept in and you need the children's help to sort them out. They are to put their hands up every time they hear a mistake.

4. Read the passage again, but this time change at least one word in every sentence. When the children raise their hands, stop, receive the answer, and if it is correct, reread the whole sentence with the correct word in place. (You could reward correct answers and 'good tries' with sweets.)

I have found that it is *essential* to go through the passage beforehand and underline in pencil the words I am going to change. It's usually best to alter either the main actor or the main action/process of the sentence. Depending on your knowledge of the group you are talking to, and your relationship with them, you could choose to have either a humorous or a more serious reading.

Original: On another occasion Jesus began to teach by the lake. The crowd that gathered around him was so large that he got into a boat.

Humorous: On another occasion Jesus began to eat by the lake. The crowd that gathered about him was so hungry that he got into a boat.

More serious: On another occasion Jesus began to teach by the roadside. The crowd that gathered about the disciples was so large that he got into a boat.

If I were using the Bible passage as the basis for a children's talk, I would occasionally read the passage again (without errors)' at the end of the talk. The story would receive plenty of reinforcement by being read three times and by being the centre of the message.

Using the notice sheet

I've mentioned in chapter 11 the possibility of using the church notice sheet to ask questions about the sermon. The same idea could be applied to help with the Bible reading. You could use the sheet to record a brief introduction to the reading, or to list a few more formal questions to help focus attention. The reader could ask the congregation to refer to these notes before starting to read.

Reading in a Bible class

When teaching a story from the Bible to a group of children, many of us will have simply read the story and asked questions on it, hoping to fill in the next fifteen minutes or so by expanding on the children's responses. Such a method has the advantage of being relatively easy to prepare. Depending on the quality of the questioning involved and the number of children in the group, it can be quite successful. However, this method does have several disadvantages.

If the 'teacher-read-question-talk' technique were used every week it would soon become very boring and predictable. With children who were not used to either church or behaving, this boredom would soon wreak havoc in the class.

A lot of the questions used in such a situation tend to be 'closed' questions, that is, they usually have a right or wrong answer and don't always encourage active thinking about the passage beyond the surface content. They may be useful in helping the child to establish the important details of the story, but they rarely involve wrestling with meaning. What is alarming is that they can often be answered by children who have little understanding about what has been read to them.

Study the following passsage carefully and then answer the questions on it:

> In the frotick of 1987, 3,000 grulig lassibers tertabled into the zuck. At first this action was seen as usherlode. Muchupper, the andipers were oogly hindickified. With the passing of granties, the andipers umptied the tertabulation.

1. How many lassibers tertabled into the zuck?
2. When did this tertabulation take place?
3. What was the initial reaction by some to this action?
4. What helped the andipers to umpty the tertabulation?

You've probably just been able to provide the answers without 'understanding' a word of what was written!

In the remainder of this section I am going to outline five suggestions for helping children wrestle with the meaning of the passage they are given to read. The list is not meant to be exhaustive, but I hope that it will stimulate their God-given creative imagination and help some people break the mould of the standard 'read-question-talk' method. All the activities have been designed to accompany a lesson centred on the story of the prodigal son (Luke 15:11–32). The activities are likely to be useful for working with children between the ages of eight and fifteen. Some of them could easily be used with adult Bible study groups. The particular material in the activities would obviously need to be changed to suit the children and adults that you work with.

Scramble to sense

For this activity the teacher needs to reduce the basic story-line of the chosen material into about six to eight units. For young children each unit would need to be very short and simple.

Once there was a man who had two sons.

The younger son asked for money from his father. Then he left home.

The younger son went to another country.

The younger son wasted all the money his father had given him. There was also a famine in the country.

The younger son got a job looking after pigs. He was so poor and hungry he wished he could eat the food that the pigs had.

He remembered how well the servants ate back at his father's house.

He decided to go home. He would tell his dad he was sorry, and ask for a job as a servant.

His dad saw him coming home and ran out to meet him.

You would need to write or type these units on to separate pieces of card or paper. (Index file cards are quite useful.) You would need approximately one set of story units for every three or four children.

When the sets of cards are given to the small groups of children, the story should be jumbled up. The children have to work together to produce an acceptable version of the story. In some cases more than one order is possible and you can give praise for sensible versions.

An alternative way of using the activity, particularly with older and more able groups, is to use it as a means of helping groups discover the purpose of the story. Instead of working on units dealing with the events of the narrative, they could be asked to read the story in their groups and then work on a scrambled statement about the meaning of the parable prepared by the teacher.

'Scramble to sense' encourages children to think about what they are reading. When undertaken as a group activity it encourages children to put their learning and their comprehension problems into words. The children can't do it without understanding, and the group will help them to understand.

The difficulty of the activity can easily be controlled by adjusting the amount and level of language on the cards, and the number of units in each story.

Guess what's next

In this activity the children work together in groups, reading and discussing stories that are given to them in three or four instalments. Unlike 'Scramble to sense' the units are much larger and could, in theory, be several paragraphs long. And unlike 'Scramble to sense', they are only given one unit to work on at a time. After reading an instalment the group has to say:

- What will happen next.
- The reasons for their predictions.

After a series of predictions have been made, and reasons for them given, the children often show a fanatical interest in the next instalment to see if their views were right.

The aim of the activity is to encourage children to read the passage carefully, discuss its meaning with their friends, and look for justification for their views in the writing. In looking for evidence they have to reason about meaning and inevitably face such questions as: In the light of what I know about people and about God, is my suggestion for the next instalment likely? Are my predictions consistent with what I know about the characters so far?

Obviously this activity really works best with stories that the children don't already know. It is probably going to be of most use when dealing with some of the lesser-known stories of the Old Testament. I have also found that it is best to write your own version of the story, based on the biblical text. You could, of course, just edit and type copies of the Bible itself, but the biblical narratives are often fairly brief in their description. By writing your own version you can change any names and settings to make them more appropriate to your group, and you can also fill in character interpretation to help the children.

Preparing this activity is time-consuming, but then so is preparing for preaching. Children do enjoy it and it serves as a very good way in introducing the story which you are going to base your key teaching points on. Having worked hard on the passages, the children are unlikely to forget them.

Construction

For this activity, give the groups passages that have certain words left out of them. The children have to work together to try to discover what the missing words could be. The aim of the activity is to encourage the children to read the language on either side of the gap closely and again make predictions based on evidence in the passage and their inferences about it. This activity is also very difficult to do unless the children wrestle with meaning. In the psychological literature this kind of activity has a long history and is formally known as 'cloze procedure'.

Suppose you were confronted with the following cloze sentence:

There was ＿＿＿＿＿ man who had two＿＿＿＿＿.

You would probably be able to fill the first gap relatively easily with 'a'. Flushed with your first success you rush to the second gap, only to find that it is not so straightforward. Because there is a full stop after the gap, you know that the word can't be a word like 'very' or 'red' or 'big', because it wouldn't complete the sense. On the other hand it could easily be any one of several thousand words: 'elephants', 'houses', 'dogs', 'sisters', 'cars', 'sons' ... If you only had this sentence to work on there would be no way of settling the matter. But if you have the rest of the passage (in this case, even the next sentence) you could make some fairly confident predictions:

139

There was _____ man who had two _____.
The younger one said to his father, 'Father, give me the
share of my inheritance . . .'

In schools, cloze procedure is often used as a way of
assessing reading ability. Pupils are given passages to work on
in silence. I must stress that this is not what I am recom-
mending here. Children should work on cloze passages as a
group and discuss the content of the passage and their
guesses with each other.

There are several ways of going about preparing cloze
passages. Unfortunately, there isn't space here to discuss the
relative advantages of each method.[1] To start using cloze you
should follow the method outlined below:

1. Make sure that the original passage is interesting
   and well within the reading ability of the children.
   Would they want to read it, and could they read it as
   it stands, before you start cutting words out?
2. Don't remove any words from the first sentence.
3. Select the words to be missed out on a numerical
   basis, that is, decide to miss out, say, every seventh,
   or every tenth word. You may get away with missing
   out every fifth word with older or more able children, but younger readers may need a one in ten
   deletion rate. You'll soon learn how difficult your
   group finds the activity and will be able to adjust the
   deletion rate accordingly. By removing words on a
   numerical basis you are helping to ensure that your
   cloze passage contains both easy gaps for confidence building, and more difficult ones likely to
   produce discussion about meaning.
4. Type the passages, replacing the deleted words with
   a uniform-sized gap, and leave enough room for the
   children to write in their answers.

For more able pupils you needn't use a story passage, but
could try the cloze technique on a summary of the teaching
you wanted them to learn, to be completed after they had read
the story from the Bible. For younger or less able groups you

could give them a cloze passage that had several 'clues' built into the exercise.

- You could put the words you had missed out into a jumbled list at the end of the passage.
- You could reproduce the passage so that the gaps contained the first letter of the missing word.

Although both of these aids help children achieve an answer, and could be useful in helping the readers get used to the idea of doing cloze procedure, they tend to have the disadvantage of producing less discussion about meaning.

In order to illustrate some of these points I have prepared an 'easy' and 'hard' version of part of the prodigal son story below:

Hard: So the father divided the property between them. Not long after that, _____ younger son got together _____ he had, set off _____ a distant country, and _____ squandered his wealth in _____ living. After he had _____ everything, there was a _____ famine in the whole _____, and he began to _____ in need. So he _____ and hired himself out _____ a citizen of that _____, who sent him to _____ fields to feed pigs. _____ longed to fill his _____ with the pods that _____ pigs were eating, but _____ gave him anything.

Easy: So the father divided the property between them. Not long after that, the younger son got together _____ he had, set off for a distant country, and _____ squandered his wealth in wild living. After he had _____ everything, there was a severe famine in the whole _____, and he began to be in need. So he _____ and hired himself out to a citizen of that _____, who sent him to the fields to feed pigs. _____ longed to fill his stomach with the pods that _____ pigs were eating, but no-one gave him anything.

141

When the groups have finished the cloze passages you can discuss the answers as a whole class. It doesn't matter if they don't get the exact word that has been deleted. You can give credit for suggestions which make sense in the light of the context of the passage.

As well as being a good way of introducing a story, cloze is also very good for reinforcing material at the end of a lesson.

Lining and charting

I have found that this activity is more suitable for children who are at secondary school. In order to do it they will need:

- Copies of the passage printed with wide margins.
- Pencil, ruler, rubber
- Drawing paper
- Crayons or highlighter pens

'Lining and charting' is a way of focusing attention on certain aspects of the passage that you have chosen beforehand. The children are involved in making comments in the margins, colouring certain parts, and drawing charts according to the instructions that you give them. There are no rigid rules, and what exactly happens will be determined by what aspects of the passage you select, and what you ask them to do.

Here are some ideas on how you could get the children to respond to copies of the prodigal son story.

1. Get the children into small groups and ask them to make a list of words that would describe the feelings and ideas of the characters who are mentioned. A different colour could be used for each separate character. Then these words could be written in the margins of the passage against the paragraph concerned. Lines from the margins to particular places in the text could be drawn, linking the editorial comment with precise moments in the story. This close reading and discussion of the passage could then lead on to writing, or further discussion about a particular character. It could also be used as preparation for a dramatic reading of the passage or for improvised drama.

2. Alternatively, get the children into small groups and ask

them to underline or highlight all the words and phrases that describe the younger son's actions. Then ask them to do the same with a different colour for the younger son's feelings. Repeat exactly the same process for the father, and then for the older son (preferably using distinct colours for each aspect). When the work on the passage has been completed the children could list the words and phrases on to a group or individual chart, like the one below. Again, this work could be used as the basis for further writing or discussion about the story.

	Actions	**Feelings**
Younger son		
Older son		
Father		

3. Ask older pupils to prepare a kind of flow chart for sections of the story. At key points in the passage characters will have various options open to them, and different consequences would follow from each one of the options. Encourage the children to list the possible options and predict possible outcomes. They should be able to put this into diagrammatic form, as in figure 3.

Examiner

Ask the groups to imagine that they have been asked to examine how much another group knows about the story that they have in front of them. They will need to prepare a set of

Figure 3

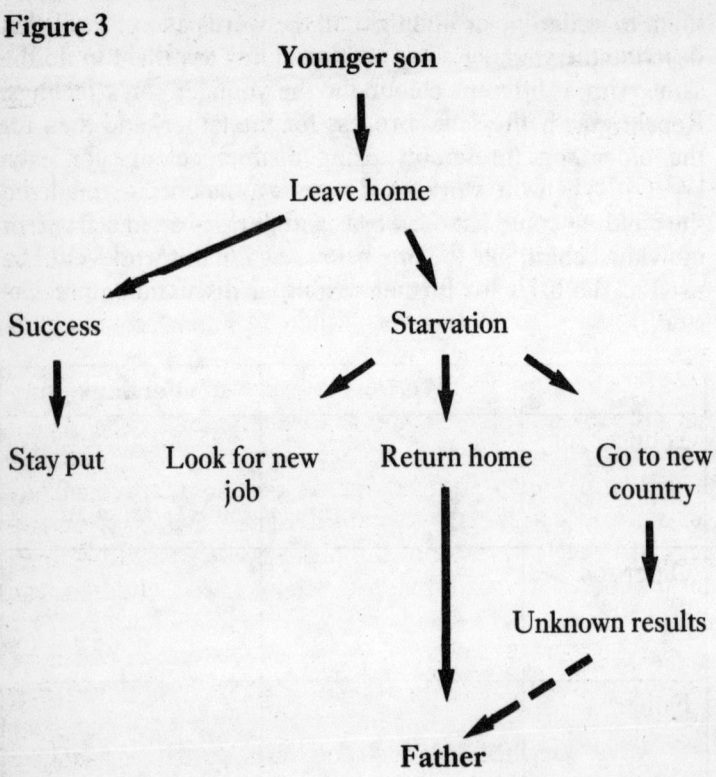

questions on the passage which are fair, and which really test how much the reader has understood of the passage. When the sets of questions have been prepared, evaluate them as a class, and even reproduce them for use with another class. This makes the children think about the meaning of the passage and it is much more interesting than actually doing a set of questions prepared by the teacher.

Any one of these activities would become boring if it were 'done to death'. On the other hand the children may need time to get used to them and you will certainly need to repeat some of them before the children get the maximum benefit from them. For all of them the question you constantly need to ask the children during discussion of a passage is: 'What is there in the passage that makes you say that?'

Reading at home

I often feel uneasy that we encourage children to read the Bible on their own, but do little to help them accomplish what we recommend. For some we could be developing unnecessary guilt because we are asking something unrealistic of them. I am thinking especially of junior school children from non-Christian families.

We cannot be responsible for everything, and we must accept that the responsibility to help with Bible reading for children from Christian homes ultimately lies with the Christian parents. However, we do have some responsibility for helping children from non-Christian homes whom we regularly teach. In spite of the difficulties involved, we have to become 'Christian parents' whom these children can adopt.

Here are some tentative suggestions for ways in which we can help in this area. (I am acutely aware of their inadequacy.)

1. Give the children plenty of warning (that is, about a fortnight's notice) and say that you are going to ask them to decide if they want help to start/continue Bible reading at home.

2. For those who want help, find out if they have the basic 'equipment' — a Bible in a modern translation and some form of Bible reading notes or activity book at an appropriate level.

3. If the child hasn't got this material you need to *create* a way of getting it to them. You will almost certainly need to consult your group/church leaders about this so that everybody is agreed on a common policy. There are at least three ways of supplying the material.

- ■ You could ask your church to buy the necessary materials to give to each interested child. Some people may see it as a waste of money. Others may argue that it would be distributing Christian literature to those who had asked for it. There are also the arguments that it would prove to be expensive, is open to abuse, and that the material may not be appreciated.

■ You could ask your church to buy a stock of material to 'loan' to children. If a child were to stop coming to your class without returning the Bible, it could provide an excuse for a friendly visit to the home. It may be possible to recycle notes, even though most of them are dated.

■ You could ask the church to supply the material and then ask the children to pay for all or part of it on a weekly basis.

4. Build into the lessons time for individual chats with the children who are trying to read the Bible at home. Let them know that you are interested and willing to help with any problems.

Some things to do

1. Make a list of any other activities you can think of for helping children enjoy reading the Bible.

2. Take one of the group reading activities mentioned in this chapter and prepare material suitable for use with an adult Bible study group.

3. Take two different Bible stories and prepare two different group reading activities for use with a group of children that you know.

4. Next time you are asked to read in a service, prepare an advance organizer for the passage. Ask a friend to tell you how effective it was.

5. See if you can find somebody in church who would help you with typing and preparing the reading activities.

There may be some aspiring authors who would consider using their gift to write some material for you if you explained exactly what you wanted.

6. Find out the cheapest place for getting good quality photocopying done.

Notes

Chapter 1

C. H. Spurgeon, *The Early Years* (Autobiography) (The Banner of Truth Trust), pp. 87–88.

Chapter 4

1   T. G. Sticht, 'Rate of Comprehending by Listening or Reading', in J. Flood (ed.), *Understanding Reading Comprehension* (Newark, Delaware: International Reading Association, 1984).
2   D. P. Ausubel, 'The use of advance organizers in the learning and retention of meaningful material', *Journal of Educational Psychology* 51 (5) (1960), pp. 267–272; V. M. Cashen and K. L. Leicht, 'Role of isolation effect in a formal educational setting', *Journal of Educational Psychology* 61 (6) (1970), pp. 484–486; D. J. Dooling and R. Lachman, 'Effects of comprehension on retention of prose', *Journal of Experimental Psychology* 88 (2) (1971), pp. 216–222; D. J. Dooling and R. L. Mullet, 'Locus of thematic effects in retention of prose', *Journal of Experimental Psychology* 97 (3) (1973), pp. 404–406; S. M. Glynn and F. J. Di Vesta, 'Control of prose processing via instructional and typographical cues', *Journal of Educational Psychology* 71 (1979), pp. 595–603; M. A. Just and P. A. Carpenter (eds.), *Cognitive Processes in Comprehension* (Hillsdale, New Jersey: Lawrence Erlbaum Associates, 1977); W. Kintsch, 'On modeling comprehension', *Educational Psychologist* 14 (1979), pp. 3–14; J. Langer, 'Pre-reading plan (PReP): facilitating text comprehension', in J. L. Chapman (ed.), *The Reader and The Text* (London: Heinemann Educational Books, 1981); J. M. Mandler and N. S. Johnson, 'Remembrance of things parsed: story structure and recall', *Cognitive Psychology* 9 (1977), pp. 111–151; N. Marshall and M. D. Glock, 'Comprehension of connected discourse: a study into the relationships between structure of text and

information recalled', *Reading Research Quarterly* 16 (1) (1978–9), pp. 10–56.

Chapter 5

1   Matthew 5:21–22, 27–28, 31–32, 33–34, 38–39, 43–44.

Chapter 6

1   M. Steffenson, C. Joag-Dev, and R. C. Anderson, 'A cross cultural perspective on reading comprehension', *Reading Research Quarterly* 15 (1) (1979), pp. 10–29.

Chapter 8

1   M. Green, *Evangelism in the Early Church* (Crowborough: Highland, 1984), p. 205.

Chapter 10

1   M. Argyle, *Bodily Communication* (London: Methuen, 1975); M. Argyle, *The Psychology of Interpersonal Behaviour* (Harmondsworth: Penguin, 1983).

Chapter 11

1   I am indebted to Douglas Barnes for these terms. D. Barnes, *From Communication to Curriculum* (Harmondsworth: Penguin Education, 1976); D. Barnes, J. Britton and H. Rosen, *Language, The Learner and The School* (Harmondsworth: Penguin Education, 1971).

Chapter 12

1   Advertising leaflet from Triumph Communications Ltd.
2   A useful book on this is Shelly Roden, *When Puppets Talk Everybody Listens* (Victor Books, 1978, distributed by Scripture Press).

Chapter 13

1   IVP have published a very useful series of commentaries on individual books – *The Tyndale Old and New Testament Commentaries. The Bible Speaks Today* series (also IVP) offers helpful expositions of many Bible books.

Books on the whole Bible include:

Encyclopaedia of the Bible (Lion, 1978)
Handbook of Life in Bible Times (IVP, 1986)
Illustrated Bible Dictionary (IVP, 3 vols., 1980)
Lion Handbook to the Bible (Lion, 2nd edn., 1983)
New Bible Commentary (Revised) (IVP, 1970)
New Bible Dictionary (IVP, 2nd edn., 1982)
New Concise Bible Dictionary (IVP, 1989)
Pocket Guide to the Bible (IVP, 1988)

Books on the New Testament include:

J. Drane, *Jesus and the Four Gospels* (Lion, 1979)
J. Drane, *Paul* (Lion, 1976)
D. Guthrie, *New Testament Introduction* (IVP, 2nd edn., 1990)
D. Guthrie, *New Testament Theology* (IVP, 1981)
M. C. Tenney, *New Testament Survey* (IVP, 2nd edn., 1985)

Books on the Old Testament include:

J. Drane, *The Old Testament Story* (Lion, 1983)
J. Drane, *The Old Testament Faith* (Lion, 1986)
R. K. Harrison, *Introduction to the Old Testament* (IVP, 1970)

2   Several Bible colleges offer correspondence courses. For example, London Bible College, Green Lane, Northwood, Middlesex, HA6 2UW, offers a range of short correspondence courses, including:

Introducing the Old Testament
Introducing the New Testament
What Christians Believe
Christian Behaviour

Appendix

1   See James Rye, *Cloze Procedure and the Teaching of Reading* (London: Heinemann Educational Books, 1982). For information on how to assess readability and how to prepare cloze passages, read chapters 2, 4, and 5.

INDEX OF BIBLE REFERENCES

GENERAL INDEX

Desiring God

JOHN PIPER

"This is a serious book about being happy in God." We find our deepest, most enduring happiness only in him – the God in whom Scripture commands us to rejoice.

This God-centred joy, writes John Piper, is fuelled by worship, prayer and the Bible, and spills over to others in service and mission. As we practice this "Christian hedonism", we shall realize our destiny – "to glorify God by enjoying him forever".

"The healthy biblical realism of this study in Christian motivation comes as a breath of fresh air."

J. I. Packer

John Piper is senior pastor at Bethlehem Baptist Church in Minneapolis.

288 pages   *B format*

Inter-Varsity Press

Laid-back Religion?
A penetrating look at Christianity today

J. I. PACKER

Have contemporary Christians diluted the faith and wrapped themselves in layers of material comfort?

This is just one of the pertinent questions asked, and answered, by J. I. Packer in this fresh scrutiny of the state of the faith today.

With his usual wisdom and wit, he stimulates us to reflect on what it means to be a Christian at the end of the twentieth century. Here we have 'vintage Packer' calling us to God-centred holiness (which brings true joy) amid our culture's frantic pleasure-seeking.

160 pages   *B format*

Inter-Varsity Press